JOSEPHUS AS AN HISTORICAL SOURCE
IN PATRISTIC LITERATURE THROUGH EUSEBIUS

Program in Judaic Studies
Brown University
BROWN JUDAIC STUDIES
Edited by
Jacob Neusner
Wendell S. Dietrich, Ernest S. Frerichs, William Scott Green,
Calvin Goldscheider, David Hirsch, Alan Zuckerman

Project Editors (Projects)

David Blumenthal, Emory University (Approaches to Medieval Judaism)
William Brinner (Studies in Judaism and Islam)
Ernest S. Frerichs, Brown University (Dissertations and Monographs)
Lenn Evan Goodman, University of Hawaii (Studies in Medieval Judaism)
William Scott Green, University of Rochester (Approaches to Ancient Judaism)
Norbert Samuelson, Temple University (Jewish Philosophy)
Jonathan Z. Smith, University of Chicago (Studia Philonica)

Number 128
JOSEPHUS AS AN HISTORICAL SOURCE
IN PATRISTIC LITERATURE THROUGH EUSEBIUS
by
Michael E. Hardwick

JOSEPHUS AS AN HISTORICAL SOURCE
IN PATRISTIC LITERATURE THROUGH EUSEBIUS

by

Michael E. Hardwick

Scholars Press
Atlanta, Georgia

JOSEPHUS AS AN HISTORICAL SOURCE IN PATRISTIC LITERATURE THROUGH EUSEBIUS

Library of Congress Cataloging in Publication Data

Hardwick, Michael E.
    Josephus as an historical source in patristic literature
    through Eusebius.
    (Brown Judaic studies ; no. 128)
    Bibliography: p.
    Includes index.
    1. Josephus, Flavius--Influence. 2. Christian literature,
Early--Sources. I. Title. II. Series
DS115.9.J6H37   1988   933'.007'2024
ISBN 1-55540-311-5 (alk. paper)   88-33715

Printed in the United States of America
on acid-free paper

To John

Contents

Acknowledgements

I thank Professor Jacob Neusner for including this volume in the Brown Judaic Studies and for a grant assisting in the cost of its publication.

The debt to my teachers and advisors, Drs. Michael J. Cook and Richard S. Sarason of the Hebrew Union College-Jewish Institute of Religion, who offered encouragement and made substantial contributions to this volume, is incalculable. Any errors in judgment are, of course, my own.

Michael E. Hardwick

Cincinnati, Ohio
January, 1988

Abbreviations

FGrH	Jacoby, F., ed. *Die Fragmente der Griechischen Historiker.*
GCS	Die griechischen christlichen Schriftsteller der ersten drei Jahrhunderten
HTR	*Harvard Theological Review*
HUCA	*Hebrew Union College Annual*
JQR	*Jewish Quarterly Review*
JSJ	*Journal for the Study of Judaism in the Persian, Hellenistic and Roman Period*
JTS	*Journal of Theological Studies*
LCL	Loeb Classical Library
MScR	*Mélanges de science religieuse*
PG	Migne, J.-P., ed. Patrologiae cursus completus. Series graeca
PL	Migne, J.-P., ed. Patrologiae cursus completus. Series latina
RHE	*Revue d'histoire ecclésiastique*
RHR	*Revue de l'histoire des religions*
RSR	*Recherches de science religieuse*
TU	Texte und Untersuchungen zur Geschichte der altchristlichen Literatur
VC	*Vigiliae christianae*
ZKG	*Zeitschrift für Kirchengeschichte*
ZWT	*Zeitschrift für wissenschaftliche Theologie*

Introduction and Methodology

Josephus occupies a place in Christian literature second only to the Bible itself in importance. For the Church, the Jewish historian has been *the* extra-biblical historical authority for the biblical and intertestamental periods as well as the history spanning the life of Jesus and the early Christian community. Further, *Against Apion* has served as a model for Christian apologetics. That Josephus came to be a dominant literary figure in Christian literature cannot be disputed and has been long recognized; however, the development of this phenomenon has been neglected. This study will document the evolution of the use of Josephus as a source by Christian authors from the period of the earliest Church to the time of Eusebius, bishop of Caesaria (d.c. 340 C.E.).

Eusebius is a watershed for Christian use of Josephus for two reasons: (1) Eusebius expanded the use of Josephan material and (2) his historical writings represent a synthesis of Christian tradition which he molded into a definition of orthodoxy with an implicit historiography that Josephus was made to serve. With regard to Eusebius' use of Josephan material, Heinz Schreckenberg notes that Eusebius belongs to that group of Church Fathers who "viewed Josephus as an authority in all questions of New Testament history and the history and religion of the Jewish people."[1] However, Schreckenberg does not go far enough in his appraisal: Eusebius does not merely find Josephus useful for all matters of historical inquiry but he was the first to do so. Further, while the bishop of Caesaria was not the first Christian writer to make use of *Against Apion,* he did introduce elements of Josephus' argument not seen before in Christian literature, and thus *C.A.* occupies a far more significant place in Christian apologetics from Eusebius onward than had been the case previously. Although the popularity of particular Josephan themes in Christian literature would wax and wane over the centuries (e.g., literature of the time of the Crusades evinces an understandably heightened interest in Josephan geography), we can say that with Eusebius Josephus became a preserve of Christian writers. Eusebius demonstrated that Josephus had something to offer on every aspect of Christian historical writing as well as on apologetics.

---

[1]H. Schreckenberg, *Die Flavius-Josephus-Tradition in Antike und Mittelalter* (Leiden, 1972), 79: "Eusebius ... gehört zu den Kirchenvätern, die Josephus als Autorität in allen Fragen der neutestamentlichen Zeitgeschichte und der Geschichte und Religion des jüdischen Volkes betrachten."

Respecting Eusebian historiography, the bishop viewed history as the arena where God works out His purposes. In developing his understanding of *Heilsgeschichte*, Eusebius utilized not only inherited Christian traditions but the gleanings of ancient historians, among them Josephus. Josephus' function was not only to illuminate history but to assist Eusebius in demonstrating the fulfillment of prophecy, particularly regarding the destruction of Jerusalem. Beginning with Eusebius, the destruction of Jerusalem as an act of divine retribution for the death of Jesus at the hands of the Jews became a common motif in Christian literature. We shall examine not only Josephus' impact on the treatment of Jerusalem in the Eusebian corpus but his contribution to the development of this treatment in earlier Christian literature.[2]

Although this particular subject has been neglected, Josephus' impact on early Christian literature has not gone unnoticed. Volume 1 of the 1726 edition of Josephus' works by Syvert Havercamp[3] begins with a list of Josephan citations in Christian literature through the tenth century C.E. The list includes Justin Martyr (pseudo-Justin), Irenaeus, Theophilus, Clement of Alexandria, Tertullian, Minucius Felix, Origen, Eusebius and Eusthathius (pseudo-Eustathius). As we shall discover, Havercamp's list of authors is not complete nor did he identify all of the Eusebian citations.

The apparatus in J.-P. Migne's *Patrologiae cursus completus. Series latina* (Paris, 1844-64) and *Series graeca* (Paris, 1857-66) also sought to deal with Josephus' impact on patristic literature. The series, however, is of uneven quality given the occasionally poor manuscript tradition and the different editors of the works included.

The series *Die griechischen christlichen Schriftsteller der ersten drei Jahrhunderte* (Leipzig and Berlin, 1897-1975) sought to correct the flaws in earlier collections of Christian writings by establishing the best possible critical texts. The apparatus includes a list of Josephan citations in Christian literature. The GCS was Heinz Schreckenberg's primary source for his catalog of Josephan citations, *Die Flavius-Josephus-Tradition in Antike und Mittelalter* (Leiden, 1972), which serves as the foundation for this dissertation. This study also rests in part upon Professor Schreckenberg's *Rezeptionsgeschichtliche und*

---

[2]In the parable of the marriage feast (Matt 22:2-14), the king, taking revenge upon those who murdered his servants, "sent his troops, destroyed those murderers and burned their city" (v. 7). That this is a reference to the destruction of Jerusalem is indisputable; however, it is not a clear reference to the death of Jesus. The servants who are killed are more likely the prophets and it is their deaths that doom the city (cf. Matt 23:37-38) for in rejecting them, the people of Jerusalem reject God. Although the destruction of Jerusalem is seen as an act of divine retribution in early Christianity, we shall discover that this does not become a common motif until Eusebius.

[3]S. Havercamp, ed., *Flavii Josephi Opera* (Amsterdam, 1726). Havercamp's edition was that used by Whiston for his translation of Josephus.

textkritische Untersuchungen zu Flavius Josephus (Leiden, 1977). My own analysis of the references which either quote or allude to Josephan material has prompted me to restrict their number more than do the GCS and Schreckenberg. Nevertheless, without them this task would have been far more difficult.

Schreckenberg's work on the transmission of Josephus' writings in late antiquity and the middle ages is an initial effort toward a replacement for Niese's dated edition of Josephus. Although Schreckenberg's purpose differs from the goal of this dissertation, both share a common need: a Josephan text superior to that of Niese. However, if the Josephan texts are less than perfect, so are the patristic texts and it is this Christian literature which contributed to the existing text-critical reconstruction of the Josephan corpus. Schreckenberg is aware that it is frequently difficult to trace the use of Josephus in late antique literature given that the Jewish historian is often used indirectly.[4] However, the problem of identifying what is an indirect use of Josephan material has been complicated, for example, by Niese's use of Eusebius to correct the single Greek text of *Against Apion,* Codex Laurentianus, from which all others are derived. Niese's preference for readings from Eusebius and the Latin version of *C.A.* over those of cod. L has somewhat predetermined our judgments regarding Eusebius' use of *Against Apion.* Unfortunately, even with a demonstrably better edition of Josephus, analysis surrounding certain possible allusions to Josephan material will remain tentative.

Scholarship on this topic is noteworthy by its absence. Although we shall encounter scholarship which deals with Josephus and individual Christian writers, little attention has been paid to Josephus' influence on Christian literature as a whole in the ante-Nicene period. G. Bardy summarizes popular Josephan themes in patristic literature and E. R. Curtius pays limited attention to Josephan themes in European literature.[5]

The individual Christian authors we shall encounter will be treated individually and themes which characterize the literature as a whole will be identified. As to the relevant texts, we shall consider any material attributed to Josephus or where Josephus is mentioned. Further, texts which show an unmistakable verbal connection to Josephan material are included. Not included are texts which share a theme with Josephus but are without any verbal similarities, or share details known beyond the Josephan corpus. An example of this is the antiquity of Moses which is a common theme in Jewish and Christian literature of late antiquity. Given the popularity of this theme and all the possible sources to which a Christian apologist might have had access, we

---

[4]H. Schreckenberg, *Die Flavius-Josephus-Tradition in Antike und Mittelalter* (Leiden, 1972), XII.
[5]G. Bardy, "Mélanges: Le souvenir de Josèphe chez les Pères," *RHE* 43 (1948), 179-191, and E. R. Curtius, *Europäische Literatur und Lateinisches Mittelalter* (Bern, 1969).

cannot draw a connection between a Christian document and *Against Apion* without clear evidence.

The dissertation nonetheless will deal with one author to whom the foregoing caveats apply: the fourth-century rhetorician Lactantius. Curtius proposed that Lactantius was familiar with Josephus' identification of the fallen "sons of God" as giants in *A.J.* 1.73 (cf. Gen 6:2). But Lactantius could just have well gleaned this tradition from Philo. I have included Lactantius in my analysis because of Curtius' suggestion and his presence in Schreckenberg's history of Josephan transmission.[6] Further, I have included all of Schreckenberg's materials referred to in the *Flavius-Josephus-Tradition* although my analysis must reject some of them.

Another criterion for inclusion in this study is that the relevant documents must date no later than 340 C.E. For this reason I have not included pseudo-Eustathius whose *Commentarius in Hexaemeron* (PG 18) contains possible references to the *Jewish War*. In that this pseudonymous commentary attributed to Eustathius (d. before 337 C.E.) clearly demonstrates use of Eusebius' *Chronicle* and the *Preparation for the Gospel*, it does not fit my criteria and is thus excluded from consideration.[7]

More complex is the case of pseudo-Justin. It is apparent that Justin Martyr (d.c. 165 C.E.) could not have been the author of the *Cohortatio ad Graecos;* however, it is not clear precisely when the document was composed. The author may have used Julius Africanus and for that reason I have treated pseudo-Justin after the African. However, it is possible that the *Cohortatio* belongs to the latter half of the fourth century and is thus not relevant to this study. For all these reasons, pseudo-Justin's witness to Josephus, like those references of dubious significance which will be encountered, must be assessed more tentatively than others.

---

[6]Schreckenberg, *Rezeptionsgeschichte und textkritische Untersuchungen zu Flavius Josephus (Leiden, 1977),* 26.

[7]See A. von Gutschmid, *Kleine Scriften* 5 (Leipzig, 1894), 598 and F. Zoepfl, *Der Kommentar des Pseudo-Eustathios zum Hexaëmeron* (Münster i.W., 1927), 24-28.

Part One

THE TEXTS

Chapter One

Theophilus Antiochenus

Little is known about Theophilus of Antioch. Eusebius (*H.E.* 4.20) states that he was the sixth bishop of Antioch from the Apostles. He gained his see in the eighth year of the reign of Emperor Marcus Aurelius (168 C.E.). His apologetical work *To Autolycus* can be dated sometime after the death of Emperor Verus (169 C.E.), given Theophilus' chronology of the emperors which ends with Verus' death (3.27). The use of the first two books of *To Autolycus* has been well documented in the western and eastern Churches although the use of the third book is not well attested. Nor can it be ascertained whether the first two books of the work circulated separately from the third.[1] However, the main use of *To Autolycus* was in the anti-Marcionite struggle for which the first two books (with their emphasis on the authority and inspiration of the Old Testament) were most suitable. The third book would not have been useful in this connection.

Book 1

Chapter(s)

1-2	Autolycus scorns Christians because of the blindness of pagans who are prevented from seeing God.
3-6	The true nature of God is known by Christianity and perceived through His works.
7-8	Faith is required to see God.
9-10	The pagan deities are immoral and absurd.
11	The king should be honored but God alone is to be worshipped.
12	The meaning of the word "Christian."
13	The Resurrection may be demonstrated by examples in nature.
14	Theophilus presents himself as an example of conversion.

---

[1] Robert M. Grant ("The Textual Tradition of Theophilus of Antioch," *VC* 6 [1952], 146-159) details the use of this work in the eastern and western Christian traditions.

Book 2

Book 3

Use of Non-Christian Writers

Theophilus' aim is to demonstrate to Autolycus the truth of the Christian message and the utter bankruptcy of the Greek traditions transmitted by the philosophers and the poets. Theophilus finds nothing in Greek philosophy which might commend itself to a Christian audience. The Gospel does not incorporate the noblest ideals of philosophy nor does Theophilus present the Gospel to Autolycus as a creed to be subjected to rational inquiry. Rather, the Christian message stands firmly opposed to Greek thought. It is not understood and accepted by Autolycus because he does not have faith. One may not become a Christian as a result of an objective and reasoned appraisal of Christianity.

With the exception of a rather lengthy citation from the Sibyl (2.36), Theophilus cites only briefly. He prefers poets to either historians or philosophers. Theophilus does provide brief citations from Homer, Hesiod, Aristophanes, Aratus, Sophocles, Simonides, Euripides, Menander the Ephesian, Thestius, Aeschylus, Pindar, Archilocus, Dionysius, Ariston, and Philemon. Further, he notes opinions of Plato, Satyrus, Herodotus, Thucydides, Pythagoras, Epicurus, Empedocles, Aesculapius, Zeno, Diogenes, Cleanthes, Critias, Protagoras of Abdera, Euhemerus, Manetho the Egyptian, and the Chaldean philosopher Berosus. With the exception of Homer and Hesiod, the author does not reveal anything but a superficial familiarity with any of the philosophers or poets.

Pagan authors are primarily guilty of writing foolish and contradictory works. Theophilus deems absurd the notion of Aristophanes that the world was hatched from an egg (2.7). Theophilus holds up this patently absurd opinion as if it were exemplary of Greek thought and by ridiculing it he aims to ridicule everything Greek. Even more significant for Theophilus, however, is the contradictory nature of the poets' and philosophers' testimony. The Greek writers cannot agree whether the world was created or was uncreated and co-eternal with the gods (2.6 and 2.8). Theophilus accuses the Greek authors of internal inconsistency:

> For the things which they declared convict them of speaking inconsistently, and the majority of them destroyed their own doctrines. For not only did they refute each other but some also annulled their own doctrines so that their fame has resulted in shame and folly. (*To Autolycus* 3.3)[2]

---

[2]Used here is the text edited by J. C. T. Otto (*Theophili Episcopi Antiocheni Ad Autolycum. Libri Tres*, Corpus Apologetarum Christianorum 8 [Jena, 1861]): Καὶ γὰρ ἃ ἔφασαν αὐτὰ ἐλέγχει αὐτούς, ἢ ἀσύμφωνα εἰρήκασιν, καὶ τὰ ἴδια δόγματα οἱ πλείους αὐτῶν κατέλυσαν · οὐ γὰρ ἀλλήλους μόνον ἀνέτρεψαν, ἀλλ᾽ ἤδη τινὲς καὶ τὰ ἑαυτῶν δόγματα ἄκυρα ἐποίησαν, ὥστε ἡ δόξα αὐτῶν εἰς ἀτιμίαν καὶ μωρίαν ἐχώρησεν ·

10 *The Texts*

Theophilus also finds the Greek poets and philosophers guilty of teaching immorality. The presentation of the Greek divinities depicts the deities as cannibals (3.5) and as indulging in incestuous relationships (3.6). To Theophilus' mind, that historians such as Herodotus could narrate an account of children being eaten by their parents serves only to promote immoral behavior: "Oh! The mind of those who thus precisely philosophized and profess philosophy! For they who taught these doctrines have filled the world with iniquity" (3.5).[3]

The final criticism leveled by Theophilus at the Greek writers is that Greek thought is too recent a development to be taken seriously. Their knowledge does not extend back in time far enough to know of the origin of the world (2.33). To illustrate this point, non-Christian writers of the East are contrasted with Greek philosophers and writers; the antiquity of the eastern authors lends them an air of authority. Berosus, a Chaldean writer from the era of Alexander the Great, is said to have instructed the Greeks in Chaldean literature (3.29). The implication is that what the Greeks know of the East is second-hand information. Not only have Greek writers been compelled to guess about history owing to the novelty of their literature, but their sinfulness has moved them to slander and abuse those who worship the God of the Christians (3.30). Antiquity is the real test for authenticity according to Theophilus. The value of writing history is to demonstrate the superior claims of Christianity owing to its inheritance of the biblical tradition which antedates Greek philosophy and literature: "Hence one can see how much more ancient and true our sacred writings are than those of the Greeks and the Egyptians or any other historians" (3.26).[4] How common a theme this is in Christian apologetic literature and how important it is to demonstrate the antiquity of Christianity will become increasingly apparent as we examine further literary examples. Suffice it to say that this theme which relates antiquity with authority and historical accuracy is a standard theme of near-eastern "anti-Greek" apologetic literature from the beginning of the Hellenistic age.

The Use of Josephus in *To Autolycus*

Josephus is treated as an unquestioned authority by Theophilus. Of particular importance is Josephus' testimony to the antiquity of the biblical tradition. He is introduced as having authored the account of the Jewish war, although what is important to Theophilus is Josephus' dating of the biblical

---

[3] ὦ τῆς διανοίας τῶν οὕτως ἀκριβῶς φιλοσοφησάντων καὶ φιλοσοφίαν ἐπαγγελλομένων! Οἱ γὰρ ταῦτα δογματίσαντες τὸν κόσμον ἀσεβείας ἐνέπλησαν.

[4] Ἐντεῦθεν ὁρᾶν ἔστιν πῶς ἀρχαιότερα καὶ ἀληθέστερα δείκνυται τὰ ἱερὰ γράμματα τὰ καθ᾽ ἡμᾶς εἶναι τῶν καθ᾽ Ἕλληνας καὶ Αἰγυπτίους, ἢ εἰ καί τινας ἑτέρους ἱστοριογράφους.

books prior to the Trojan war. They antedate and are thereby more illustrious than the works of Homer or the great lawgivers of Greek culture (3.23).

Of all the Josephan corpus, Theophilus is most interested in and most influenced by *Against Apion*. Theophilus develops his argument for the greater antiquity of the biblical tradition in the third book of *To Autolycus*. He follows *C.A.* quite closely with regard to overall content although he summarizes certain sections rather freely . In 3.20, Theophilus makes use of *C.A.* 1.93-102, in which Josephus cites the Egyptian historian Manetho's chronology of the pharaohs from the Exodus to Rameses. For both Theophilus and Josephus, the purpose of the citation from Manetho is to demonstrate the great antiquity of Moses. Manetho's chronology demonstrates that the Exodus preceded the Trojan war by almost 1000 years (3.21 and *C.A.* 1.104). Other, less flattering, statements by Manetho regarding the origin of the Hebrews are dismissed by both Theophilus and Josephus.

Both Theophilus and Josephus turn to Tyrian evidence for the antiquity of Solomon's Temple (3.22 and *C.A.* 1.106-126). The construction of the Temple is set at 143 years and 8 months before the founding of Carthage by the Tyrians. Both authors provide the chronology of the Tyrian kings from Hiram, friend and fellow monarch of Solomon, to Pygmalion, whose sister built Carthage.

Theophilus continues with a biblical chronology from Adam to the Babylonian captivity (3.24-25) and the chronology of the Roman emperors (3.27). He prefaces each chronology (3.23 and 26) with the declaration that the Greek literature is too recent a development to pretend mastery of these historical events. The Phoenician, Egyptian, and especially the Hebrew writings are authoritative owing to their greater antiquity. Josephus does not provide a biblical chronology in *Against Apion* but refers his readers to *A.J.* (which is the Josephan chronology) for the history of the Hebrews prior to the erection of the Temple (*C.A.* 1.127).

Theophilus follows the major points of Josephus' history of the Babylonian captivity, the rise of the Persian empire under Cyrus, and the rebuilding of the Temple under Darius (3.25 and *C.A.* 1.128-154). The Chaldean historian Berosus, who is said to have introduced Chaldean literature and history to the Greeks, is important because his witness supports aspects of the biblical testimony concerning the Flood, the exile, and the Persian period (3.29 and *C.A.* 1.128ff.).

Josephus and the Text of *To Autolycus*

Codex Marcianus (Venetus graecus), the oldest extant text of *To Autolycus*, belongs to the tenth or eleventh century. Although Theophilus was read in both the eastern and western branches of the Church, little is known of the transmission of *To Autolycus*.[5] Therefore, it is not possible to say anything definitive regarding the text of *C.A.* used by Theophilus. There are omissions and inconsistencies in the Venice manuscript, possibly scribal errors occurring during transmission, which make the document of dubious value for the history of *C.A.*. Nevertheless, Niese utilized the edition of J. Otto, based upon Codex Marcianus, in his critical apparatus.[6]

Part of the problem in comparing *To Autolycus* with *C.A.* is that Theophilus does not cite the Josephan material but follows it rather freely. For example, Josephus does not recite the biblical chronology from the Exodus to the Babylonian Exile but refers the reader to *A.J.* (*C.A.* 1.127). Theophilus, however, interpolates a lengthy recitation of biblical chronology (3.24 and 25) into material drawn from *C.A.*. Further, *C.A.* includes a lengthy citation from Berosus on Babylonian history (*C.A.* 1.134-141) which is omitted by Theophilus. More problematic, however, than his free use of Josephan material are internal inconsistencies and discrepancies with *C.A.* when Theophilus is following Josephus closely.

A major discrepancy between *To Autolycus* and *C.A.* involves the list of pharaohs and the lengths of their reigns. The list is as follows:

C.A.	To Autolycus (Venice ms)[7]
Tethmosis, 25 years, 4 months	Moses (corr. Tethmosis), same
Chebron, 13 years	same
Amenophis, 20 years, 7 months	same
Amesses 21 years, 9 months	Amesse, 21 years, 1 month
Mephres, 12 years, 9 months	same
Mephramouthosis, 25 years, 10 months	Mephrammouthosis, 20 years, 10 months
Thmosis, 9 years, 8 months	Tuthmoses, same
Amenophis, 30 years, 10 months	Damphenopis, same
Orus, 36 years, 5 months	same
daughter, 12 years, 1 month	same 10 years, 3 months

[5]*ilid*. Although *To Autolycus* was widely read, the citations are inadequate to reconstruct a history of its transmission. Therefore, the Venice manuscript remains the best witness in that the other mss., the Paris and the Bodleian, are based upon it.
[6]B. Niese, *Flavii Iosephi Opera. Edidit et apparatu critico instruxit* (Berlin, 1889), 5:ix.
[7]Otto's edition is based upon the Venice manuscript. As this is the primary text, its readings are given. The correction in the first listing is Otto's based upon a marginal reading in the Bodleian manuscript. Otto follows the traditional corrected reading in earlier editions of the text.

Rathotis, 9 years	absent
Akencheres, 12 years, 5 months	absent
Akencheres, 12 years, 3 months	Mercheres, same
Armais, 30 years, 1 month	same, 4 years, 1 month
Rameses, 1 year, 4 months	same
Armesses Miamoun, 66 years, 2 months	Messes Miammou, same
Amenophis, 19 years, 6 months	same
Sethos-Ramesses (no years)	Thoissos and Ramesses, 10 years

Citing Manetho, Josephus (*C.A.* 1.94-103) lists eighteen monarchs who reigned a total of 393 years. *To Autolycus,* however, contains ten discrepencies in the names of the pharaohs and five differences with regard to the length of their reigns.[8] The errors in name range from mere errors in spelling to omission of two monarchs found the Josephan list. Further, *To Autolycus* 3. 21 notes that the total figure for all the reigns is 313 years which is incorrect. The Venice manuscript of *To Autolycus* is to be corrected because Tertullian (*Apolog.*19), who read *To Autolycus*, agrees with the 393 years of *C.A.*[9]

A similar discrepancy involves the chronology from Hiram to Pygmalion (3.22 and *C.A.* 1.117-126):

C.A.	To Autolycus
Heiromos, 34 years	same (reign not given)
Balbazeros, 17 years	same
Abdastaptos, 9 years	absent
Methousastartos, 12 years	same
Astharumos, 9 years	same
Phelletos, 8 months	Helles, same
Eithobalos, 32 years	Iouthobalos, same
Balezoros, 6 years	Bazoros, same
Mettenos, 29 years	same
Pygmalion, 47 years	same, 7 years

Not only is there inconsistency with respect to the Josephan list but Theophilus' total number of years between the beginning of Hiram's reign and the founding of Carthage does not agree with the numbers in his list. Since Theophilus could follow Josephus quite closely and accurately, it seems likely that the discrepancies are the result of scribal error during transmission of the

---

[8] Although Josephus does not include the length of Sethos-Ramesses' reign, he includes a figure of 10 years for it in his total.

[9] Robert M. Grant ("Notes on the Text of Theophilus, To Autolycus III," *VC*-12 [1958], 136-144) compares the third book of the Theophilan Venice manuscript with Codex Laurentianus which is the sole Greek manuscript of *C.A.*

text rather than an error during composition.[10] Nevertheless, the state of the Venice manuscript makes it of little value for the history of the transmission of *C.A.* except as an example of how texts can be corrupted by scribal error.

Summary

The central point in Theophilus' argument against Greek thought is the antiquity of biblical traditions which antedate both hellenistic philosophy and poetry. In making this argument, Josephus is his primary source who offered not only chronological material but, in *Against Apion,* provided a fully developed argument as to the greater antiquity and hence superiority of biblical literature over against Greek philosophical and literary traditions. Interestingly, Theophilus did not deem it necessary to provide a link between the biblical traditions of the Jews and the Church. That Christianity was the heir to Jewish antiquity is assumed. The need to prove this thesis will surface, however, in other literature we shall encounter before the Church's ownership of biblical tradition is settled.

---

[10]*ibid.,* 139 and 140. Grant notes that the Venice manuscript in consistent with regard to mathematical error. Theophilus' chronologies are generally problematic.

Chapter Two

Melito of Sardis

We learn from Eusebius that Melito of Sardis was active in the eighth year of the reign of Marcus Aurelius (168 C.E.; *H.E.* 6.19 and 20). Melito is said to have been writing during the proconsulate of Servilius Paulus (*H.E.* 4.26), although the latter is not known. Melito was a contemporary of Hegesippus, Apollinarus and Irenaeus (*H.E.* 6.20), and was involved in the Quartodeciman controversy which addressed the problem of whether the Paschal festival should be observed on the fourteenth of Nisan or on the following Sunday, to emphasize the Resurrection. Melito followed the traditional practice of observance on the fourteenth of Nisan rather than the later custom (*H.E.* 5.24). He was bishop of Sardis and the author of numerous works. Eusebius provides a bibliography of which only fragmentary evidence is extant (*H.E.* 4.26). Nothing else is known of Melito except that he was celibate (*H.E.* 5.24), was purported to be a prophet (Jerome, *De viris illustribus* 24) and was buried in Sardis (*H.E.* 5.24).

Melito's works were initially known only through fragments.[1] In 1936, however, some leaves of the Chester Beatty papyri were recognized to be a work on the Passion by Melito.[2] C. Bonner identified the leaves as *On the Passion*. The text does not have a title but μελειτων stands at the beginning of the homily. Bonner established the title of the work by a sentence (recognized as section 96 of the Chester Beatty ms) used by Anastasius of Sinai and attributed to that work.[3] Another Greek document in the Bodmer papyrus codes was later recognized as being the same work; it included the title ΜΕΛΙΤΩΝΟΣ ΠΕΡΙ

---

[1]J.C.T. Otto, *Hermiae Philosophi Irrisio Gentilium Philosphorum. Apologetarum Quadrati, Aristides, Aristonis, Miltiadis, Melitonis, Apollinaris Reliquiae,* Corpus Apologetarum Christianorum 9 (Jena, 1872), 374-478.
[2]S.G. Hall, *Melito of Sardis. On Pascha and Fragments* (Oxford, 1979), xvii-xix. Hall documents the discovery and identification of the mss.
[3]C. Bonner, *The Homily on the Passion by Melito of Sardis with Some Fragments of the Apocryphal Ezekiel,* Vol. 12 of Studies and Documents, ed. K. Lake and S. Lake (London, 1940), 7.

ΠΑΣΧΑ.[4] On these grounds the work has been identified as being *On the Passion* mentioned by Eusebius (*H.E.* 4.26).

A problem exists in that Eusebius refers in that passage to τὰ περὶ τοῦ πάσχα δύο. He may be referring to two different books or to one in two parts. Our text, however, is a single work which does not lend itself to a division in terms of content. Further, Eusebius cites an introductory line from *On the Passion* which is not found in our texts. It has been suggested that our *On the Passion* is not that by Melito[5] or that it is not to be identified as the same work.[6] Perler suggested that the present work was the first part of a larger work and the introductory line cited by Eusebius could very well have been a scribal emendation and not part of the original text.[7] Hall proposed that the present work be divided into two parts, a suggestion which he defended from his analysis of the Georgian version of the text and Jewish evidence.[8] Therefore, the relationship between our text entitled *On the Passion* and that cited by Eusebius cannot be known for certain.

Hall, in his edition of the work, points out that, although we cannot know that our text is that mentioned by Eusebius, there are good reasons for assuming that it is by Melito. The rhetorical forms employed by the author are consistent with those used by second-century Asian orators. Second, the style and tone of *On the Passion* are consistent with the fragments attributed to him. Citations from the Bible are generally from the Old Testament which conforms to earlier rather than later practice. The debate with the Marcionites over the status of the Old Testament seems to be in the author's mind and Eusebius informs us of Melito's defense of orthodoxy. There are indications that the author knew the Gospel of Peter which would be more likely before 200 C.E. than later. There appears to be some acquaintance with Jewish paschal tradition which comports with Melito's position in the Quartodeciman debate.[9]

Sentence(s):

1-4   The Passover is presented as an eternal event rather than a historical one. Melito presents the burial and resurrection as having been foreshadowed by the Passover.

---

[4]M. Testuz, ed., *Papyrus Bodmer XIII, Méliton de Sardes Homélie sur la Pâque*, Bibliotheca Bodmeriana (Geneva, 1960).

[5]P. Nautin, "L'homélie de 'Méliton' sur la passion," *RHE* 44 (1949), 429-438 and *Le Dossier d'Hippolyte et de Méliton*, Patristica I (Paris, 1953), 53-55.

[6]J. Blank, *Meliton von Sardes Vom Passa, Die älteste christliche Osterpredigt*, Sophia 3 (Freiburg im Breslau, 1963), 14-15.

[7]O. Perler, *Ein Hymnus zur Ostervigil von Meliton? Papyrus Bodmer XII*, Paradosis 15 (Freiburg, 1960), 19-20.

[8]S. G. Hall, "Melito in the light of the Passover Haggadah," *JTS* n.s. 22 (1971), 29-46.

[9]S. G. Hall, *Melito of Sardis*, xix.

5-10   The Paschal lamb is really the Christ.

11-35   Melito summarizes the events surrounding the Passover as recorded in Scripture. However, it was not the blood of the sheep which spared Israel but the Spirit of the Lord.

36-47a   The Law was but a foreshadow of the Gospel.

47b-104   The origin of sin is presented and the wickedness of humankind is described. Christ defeated sin and death by his death and resurrection which is the true Passover.

"On the Passion" and Josephus

Melito's work is a typological interpretation of the Passover event. The various elements of the Passover account are depicted as foreshadowings of the death and resurrection of Christ. Melito cites the Old Testament several times.[10] Generally, the author summarizes the biblical text. Melito's use of the New Testament is obscure. His statements regarding Christ could be derived from the teaching of the Church rather than from reflections upon the New Testament.[11]

Melito does not cite any material other than the Bible. Melito traces the history of humankind from Adam on in order to show the necessity for the Christ event (47-71). Apparently reflecting upon Scripture, the author depicts a race doomed to death owing to sin and in need of deliverance. It was only in Christ that the Passover, that deliverance, was fulfilled. In his depiction of a race destroyed by its own lust and corruption, Melito notes that, in addition to lust, tyranny, and murder, people were driven to cannibalism (52). Melito may be alluding to Josephus' account of the siege of Jerusalem in *B.J.* 6 and particularly to the story of a mother caught devouring her child (6.201-213). Although there are accounts in Scripture of cannibalism during times of siege (Deut 28:53-57, 2 Kgs 6:28-29), Perler noted similarity with *B.J.* 6.193-213 in his commentary on *On the Passion*.[12] Lam 4:10, which Origen probably saw as foreshadowing the later siege of Jerusalem (*Comm. Lam.* 105) and which he related to *B.J.* 6, may be what Melito had in mind. Although one cannot say with certainty that Josephus' account of the Roman siege of Jerusalem was in

---

[10]Gen 2:16-17 in section 47, Deut 28:66 in 61, Ps 2:1-2 in 62, Ps 17:14 at 98, Isa 3:10 in 72, Isa 50:8 in 101, Isa 53:7-8 in 64; Jer 63. For a comparison of the citations to the LXX see C. Bonner, 36-45.

[11]Matt 17:24 in section 86, Matt 27:24 in 92, Matt 27:34 in 79. Bonner notes that the two latter references can also be found in the Gospel of Peter. Bonner further notes several possible allusions to the Pauline corpus, Hebrews, and the Apocalypse. He admits, however, that the language may be part of the general vocabulary of the period (pp. 40-41).

[12]O. Perler, *Méliton de Sardes. Sur la Pâque et Fragments,* Sources Chrétiennes (Paris, 1966), 164-165.

Melito's mind, elements in Melito's text reflect the situation in *B.J.* rather than what we find in Scripture. First, the situation is one of oppression and slavery (49) and yet the murders, bloodshed, and lawlessness are not of foreign origin but are the sins of the people (50). In the biblical stories the great horror is cannibalism brought on by a siege. For Melito, however, cannibalism is only the crowning horror to the sins of the people. In *B.J.* 6, Josephus draws a picture of a suffering Jerusalem which is being tyrannized not by the Romans but by Jewish parties competing for control of Jerusalem. The cannibalism described by Josephus is the ultimate tragedy as it is for Melito.

If Melito is reflecting upon the Josephan account of Jerusalem's siege and destruction by the Romans, he does not link this event with the notion of Jewish guilt for the crucifixion of Christ. Melito does accuse the Jews of ingratitude, for they received much from God and yet killed the Christ (88-99). If the connection did not occur to him, it would to later writers.

Chapter Three

Minucius Felix

The *Octavius* by the Roman lawyer, Marcus Minucius Felix, is an apology for Christianity in the form of a dialogue between the Christian Octavius and the pagan Caecilius on a trip from Rome to Ostia. Minucius Felix serves as moderator and narrator of the dialogue. Nothing is known of Minucius Felix except that he was a jurist prior to his conversion to Christianity[1] and no other literature can be attributed to him.

Chapter(s)

1   Minucius Felix recalls his friend Octavius, now deceased, and proceeds to tell about his conversation with Caecilius whom he converted to Christianity.

2   Minucius Felix, Octavius, and Caecilius journey from Rome to the sea. Octavius opens a debate with Caecilius who does homage to an image of Serapis.

3-15   Caecilius argues in favor of the Roman religion. His main criticisms of Christians and Christianity are: (1) Christians have opinions on matters about which they are not sufficiently educated. (2) The Roman religion is responsible for the considerable success of the Empire and one should not reject what has made that success possible. (3) Christians are not socially respectable and hold ridiculous beliefs. (4) Christians engage in idle speculation about matters not knowable by mortals.

16-38   Octavius responds to Caecilius. The major points of his argument are: (1) Reason has been given to all men and Providence reveals itself in the world at large. Therefore, Christians are capable of pondering the mysteries of God. (2) That our ancestors have followed certain superstitions is no reason to continue doing so. Roman religion is a collection of superstitions which are not taken seriously even by Romans. (3) Roman success is not the result of the Roman deities but a consequence of efficient cruelty. (4)

---

[1]Jerome, *De Viris Illus.* 100.58.

Criticism of Christianity is demonic in origin and is based upon incorrect assumptions and half-truths. Octavius corrects a number of Caecilius' misinterpretations of Christian doctrine.

39-40   Caecilius is convinced by Octavius' argument and is converted to Christianity.

Date and Relationship to Tertullian's Apology

Dating this work with any certainty is a difficult task. Harnack went so far as to declare it a hopeless one.[2] However, it is possible to ascertain a reasonable *terminus a quo*. In chapters 9 and 21 reference is made to Fronto of Cirta although it cannot be said whether Fronto is still living at the time of Minucius' writing. We will accept, therefore, Harnack's earliest possible date of 160 C.E. assuming that the work may have been written during the last years of Fronto's life.[3]

Regarding the *terminus ad quem*, it is quite probable that Novatian, who was active in the middle of the third century C.E., employed the *Octavius* in his *De Trinitate*.[4] Further, Beaujeu discovered parallels which indicate Cyprian's dependence upon the *Octavius*.[5] The alleged parallels range from the plausible to the seemingly certain. There is further dependence upon the *Octavius* by the pseudo-Cyprianic *Ad Novatianum*. Internal evidence indicates that it was composed sometime after the persecution of the Church by Gallus and Volusion (251-253 C.E.).[6] Thus we can posit a *terminus ad quem* of c. 260 C.E.

A more difficult problem concerns the relationship between the *Octavius* and Tertullian's *Apology* and *To the Nations (Ad Nationes)*. *To the Nations* was written sometime before the *Apology* and material from the former work can be found in the latter. If Minucius knew Tertullian's work, it is not necessary that he would have read *To the Nations* but he need have only known the *Apology*. However, if dependence goes the other way, Tertullian made use of the *Octavius* for both his works.[7] The difficulty of resolving this problem is reflected by the volume of literature on it. We can, however, narrow the scholarship to three

---

[2]A. Harnack, *Die Chronologie der altchristlichen Literatur bis Eusebius* (Leipzig, 1904), 2:324.

[3]*Ibid*. Fronto lived from c. 100 to c. 170 C.E.

[4]Jerome (*De Viris Illus*. 70) had identified Tertullian as the source for Novation but Harnack, *ibid.*, demonstrated that Novation's argument on the nature of God follows that of Minucius Felix rather than that of Tertullian's *Adversus Praxeam*.

[5]J. Beaujeu, *Minucius Felix: Octavius* (Paris, 1964), lxvii-lxviv.

[6]Beaujeu, lxvii-lxviv.

[7]Beaujeu, liv-lv. Beaujeu provides a complete list of the parallels between Minucius Felix and Tertullian.

positions: (1) Tertullian made use of the *Octavius;* (2) Minucius Felix utilized Tertullian; (3) both authors employed a common source.

The priority of Minucius Felix was first asserted in modern times by de Muralto in 1836.[8] However, it was not until A. Ebert published *Tertullians Verhältnis zu Minucius Felix* (Leipzig, 1868) that priority of Minucius Felix was given serious defense. Ebert's position was based upon what he considered the consistency of those passages shared by Tertullian and Minucius Felix with the overall purpose of the *Octavius.* Ebert viewed Tertullian's *Apology* as reflecting a hasty composition and being juridical in approach whereas those passages shared by the two authors are philosophical in nature and therefore more likely original with Minucius Felix. L. Massebieau[9] and P. Monceaux[10] followed Ebert's method but arrived at a different result. They concluded that Minucius copied material from Tertullian who was the more vigorous and therefore more creative writer. Minucius Felix was the rhetorician who made use of the *Apology* which was the product of the more creative intellect. R. Heinze[11] made an exhaustive and exact study of the relevant passages and concluded that Minucius Felix abstracted material from the *Apology* and simplified it for effect. For Heinze, that the passages in the *Apology* are less pointed does not detract from the more logical order by Tertullian. B. Axelson[12] proposed that Minucius Felix edited his already complete manuscipt after reading *To the Nations* and the *Apology.*

It has also been proposed that both Tertullian and Minucius Felix made use of a common source.[13] However, this proposal has not received broad acceptance given that it is necessary to propose and describe in detail a work for whose existence there is no evidence other than that of Tertullian and Minucius Felix.

If Tertullian made use of the *Octavius* then we could establish a *terminus ad quem* of 200 C.E. If, however, the prevailing opinion of Tertullian's primacy is correct, the earliest date of the *Octavius* would be c. 200 C.E. The problem is

---

[8]Jerome (*De Viris Ill.* 53 and *Ep.* 70.5) gives Tertullian priority although his chronology is not above suspicion. For an extensive survey of the scholarship on the relationship between Tertullian and Minucius Felix, see H. J. Baylis, *Minucius Felix and his Place among the Early Fathers of the Latin Church* (London, 1928), 274-359. For a more recent treatment see J. Beaujeu, liv-lxvii.
[9]"L'Apologetique de Tertullien et L'Octavius de Minucius Felix," *RHR* 15 (1887), 316-346.
[10]*Histoire litteraire de l'Afrique chretienne depuis les origines jusqu'à l'invasion arabe* (Paris, 1901), 1:316-346.
[11]*Tertullians Apologeticum* (Leipzig, 1910).
[12]*Das Prioritätsproblem Tertullian-Minucius Felix* (Lund, 1941).
[13]F. Wilhelm, "De Min. Fel. Oct. et Tert. Apol." in *Breslauer philol. Abhandl.* 2 (1887). Wilhelm, following a suggestion made by W. von Hartel in 1869, developed the theory that the common source contained material from Cicero used by both authors.

the inconclusiveness of proof. The priority of Minucius Felix rests upon the coherence and style of his narrative while Tertullian's priority depends upon the assumption that his is the more vigorous and therefore more creative work. Both sides employ a priori considerations regarding what characterizes creativity. Therefore, the results are predetermined. Given the state of the debate it is not wise to go beyond dating the *Octavius* between c. 160 and c. 250 C.E.

Minucius and His Literary Sources

Minucius Felix is rather spartan in his use of Scripture. Beaujeu noted possible allusions to the Old Testament: Genesis in chapters 19 and 32, Exodus in 33, Kings in 32, Job in 17 and 36, Psalms in 32, Isaiah in 32, and Jeremiah in 29. He further isolated possible references to New Testament materials: Luke in chapter 36, John in 19, Acts in 32, Romans in 31, I and II Corinthians in 31, I Timothy in 29 and 32, and II Peter in 34. These allusions reflect subject matter rather than any clear literary dependence.[14] Therefore, one might just as well suppose that Minucius Felix is drawing from the common parlance of the Church rather than directly from the Bible.

If his dependence upon Scripture is limited (if not entirely lacking), Minucius' use of Latin literature is ample. Beaujeu noted his dependence upon Seneca and especially Cicero's *De Natura Deorum* for meter, form and content (chapters 5, 17, 18, 19, and isolated passages throughout the work). Minucius Felix makes use of the *Academica* (chapter 13), *De Amicitia* (3 and 21), *De Finibus* (14 and 17), *De Legibus* (20), *De Republica* (33), *Tusculanae Disputationes* (17), *Brutus* (1), *De Oratore* (1), *De Inuentione* (18), *Verrines* (11 and 15), *De Imperio Cn. Pompei* (10), *Pro Milone* (32) and *Ad Atticum* (1).[15] Beaujeu also notes that, next to Cicero, Seneca is most often cited: *Dialogi* (chapter 36), *Consol. ad Heluiam* (19), *Ad Marciam* (6), *Ad Polybium* (11), *Epistolae Morales* (10, 11, 14, 16, 24, 32, 36, 40) and traces of other works. Also found are citations from Sallust (14 and 40), Valerius Maximus (36), Tacitus (8), Suetonius (3) along with citations from poets such as Homer (19), Ennius (12 and 19), Lucretius (2 and 5), Catalus (3), Juvenal (4), Statius (18) and epecially Virgil (3, 5-7, 12, 13, 19, 23, 25, 35, 36).[16]

Minucius' dependence upon Latin literature and his neglect of biblical material could be construed as ignorance of Scripture, yet his purpose is to offer a credible defense of Christianity to Romans using language and concepts familiar to them. Citing Scripture to those who denied its validity would have been a futile effort. The use of Scripture would have made the *Octavius* a didactic work for Christians who required a response to pagan accusations rather than an apology for Christianity to those who misunderstood its teachings. To

---

[14]Beaujeu, xxxvii.
[15]Beaujeu, xxxii-xxxiii.
[16]Beaujeu, xxxiv-xxxv.

those who deem Minucius Felix a rhetorician rather than a philosopher, it should be emphasized that he follows Cicero in thinking that to speak elegantly and eloquently on a subject is part of the philosopher's task.

Minucius' use of Josephus is part of his attempt to ground his opinion in an authority recognized by all. In chapter 33 Minucius Felix responds to the Roman charge that the destruction of the Jewish nation proves the superiority of the Roman deities to the biblical God. Minucius Felix does not reject the logic and indeed supports it by disassociating the Jews from Christianity and from the protection of God. The fate of the Jewish people did not come from the inefficacy of God but from their abandonment of Him: "Thus you will understand that they abandoned before they were abandoned and they were not, as you impiously say, taken captive with their God, but were given up by God as deserters from His discipline."[17] Josephus is mentioned, not as Jewish authority who witnesses against his own people, but as an authority on the Jewish war recognized by his Roman audience along with Antonius Julianus. Josephus' own criticisms of the Jewish defenders at the siege of Jerusalem, which could be utilized for Minucius Felix' argument, are interestingly absent. Although his knowledge of Latin literature is extensive, Minucius Felix demonstrates little acquaintance with Greek writing. One wonders whether he read Josephus at all or is merely mentioning the name of a famous historian who wrote about the Jews.

---

[17]*Oct.* 33.5 (Beaujeu's ed.): "Ita prius eos deseruisse comprehendes quam esse desertos nec, ut impie loqueris, cum deo suo captos sed a deo ut disciplinae transfugos deditos."

Chapter Four

Irenaeus

Irenaeus ranks as the most significant theologian of the Christian West in the second century. He was born in Asia Minor and was a student of Polycarp (*H.E.* 5.20). He served as priest and later bishop in Lyons during the reigns of Marcus Aurelius and Commodus. His writings are chiefly doctrinal in nature: he was greatly concerned to demonstrate the errors of Gnosticism and the apostolic authority of the Church.

The only extant witness in Irenaeus to Josephus is a Greek fragment collected by Massuet (fragment 33 in PG 7:1245-1248). Given the context, the fragment appears to be part of an exegetical piece on Numbers. Irenaeus notes that, according to Josephus (*A.J.* 2.238-253), Moses was raised in Egyptian palaces and married an Ethiopian princess after being aided by her in defeating the Ethiopian forces. Irenaeus does not betray more than a superficial knowledge of the account of Moses' life in the *A.J.* and it is not possible to say whether his knowledge was gained directly or from a secondary source.

Irenaeus did make use of doxographical materials in his *Against Heresies* (*Adversus Haereses;* PG 7:438-1224). Irenaeus followed a common practice among Christian writers in utilizing a summary of various philosophers and philosophical schools. H. Diels demonstrated that the particular work from which he drew was originally written in the Augustan period by Aetius and subsequently underwent several revisions. The version used by Irenaeus is one attributed to Pseudo-Plutarch.[1] Irenaeus makes it clear in the *Against Heresies* that he believes that the Gnostics (whose positions he will refute) drew the framework for their system from philosophy. Therefore, Irenaeus is not favorably inclined toward philosophy but considers it to be a vain pursuit. However, it should not be assumed that Irenaeus was totally ignorant of philosophical literature for he does demonstrate a knowledge of rhetoric. W. Schoedel analyzed the structure of *Against Heresies* and noted that it generally coincides with hellenistic rhetorical models and appears especially close to those described by Cicero.[2] R. M. Grant noted that Irenaeus demonstrates knowledge

---

[1]H. Diels, *Doxographi Graeci* (Berlin, 1879), 170ff.
[2]W.R. Schoedel, "Philosophy and Rhetoric in the *Adversus Haereses* of Irenaeus," *VC* 13 (1959), 27-31.

of Homer, Aesop's fables, Menander, Antiphanes, Sophocles, Pindar, and Stesicorus. Although Irenaeus denies any rhetorical skill, these authors were part of a rhetorician's education.[3] Irenaeus betrays some knowledge of philosophy despite his assertions to the contrary. Indeed, his pretended ignorance could be viewed as a rhetorical device to emphasize his denigration of philosophy. Irenaeus' knowledge of philosophy and literature was probably general and derived from some education in rhetoric.

Given Josephus' reputation as a historian, it is not surprising that Irenaeus mentions Josephus in connection with Moses. The particular tradition mentioned is hardly Josephan in origin (Josephus may have derived his information from Artapanus or we are dealing with what became a common Alexandrian theme by Josephus' time of which the sole extant literary witness is Artapanus) and we cannot say for certain that Irenaeus was familiar with anything more than the fact that Josephus wrote about Moses and his Ethiopian campaign. Given his use of doxographical materials in the *Against Heresies,* it is quite possible that his knowledge of Josephus was secondhand as well.

---

[3]R.M. Grant, "Irenaeus and Hellenistic Culture," *HTR* 42 (1949), 48-51.

Chapter Five

Clement of Alexandria

Titus Flavius Clemens, better known as Clement of Alexandria, taught in a catechetical school in Alexandria (Eusebius, *H.E.* 5.11). We know but few facts of his life except that he was possibly a priest (*H.E.* 6.11.6). His greatest significance lies in the attempt to express the Christian faith in philosophical terms. His penchant for philosophy is reflected also in the writings of his intellectual heirs (of whom Origen and Eusebius are of interest here), whose theological speculations would put them in conflict with established orthodoxy. Nevertheless, Clement's acceptance of philosophy as a worthwhile enterprise and his own erudition have left an indelible mark on the Church.

The *Stromata* (Στρωμστεῖς) or *Miscellanies* is a difficult work to categorize except as a series of musings on the Christian faith.[1] Owing to its fragmentary nature, the *Miscellanies* refuse to be dated. Whether the document was completed at one time or was completed in two or more parts is uncertain. Further, it is unclear whether the *Miscellanies* was written while Clement was in Alexandria or after his departure. The work was most likely composed at the end of the second century or at the end of the first decade of the third century C.E.[2]

Outline

Book

1   Clement portrays philosophy as the servant of theology and valuable for a correct understanding of Scripture. However, sophistry (whose ends are other than seeking the truth) stands in contrast to philosophy which has attained some measure of truth

---

[1] Otto Stählin, ed., *Clemens Alexandrinus. Zweiter Band. Stromata Buch I-VI*, GCS 15 (Leipzig, 1906). Stählin prepared a second edition of the volume whose publication was prevented by the war. After Stählin's death, a third edition was prepared by L Früchtel and published as GCS 52 (Berlin, 1960). This third edition of Stählin's work is used here.

[2] A summary of the scholarship on this question can be found in Elizabeth A. Clark, *Clement's Use of Aristotle: The Aristotelian Contribution to Clement of Alexandria's Refutation of Gnosticism* (New York, 1977), 92-94.

even in pagan hands. Clement traces the antiquity of the Jews and outlines the life of Moses whose philosophy was borrowed by Plato.

2   Knowledge of God can only be gained through faith which makes philosophy possible. Clement analyzes different kinds of knowledge and asserts that the Mosaic code was the source for the Greek ethical system. Gnostic philosophy is examined as are the opinions of various Greek philosophers on the chief Good.

3   Clement condemns the Basilidians and those like them who made celibacy a requirement rather than a divine gift.

4   Martyrdom is praised as a witness to Christ, but the Basilidians, who actively seek martyrdom, are criticized. The Christians are to seek the common good in life by living as well as dying as martyrs if necessary, but are not to seek death. Both men and women are capable of perfection (in contrast to the Gnostic doctrine which excludes women from perfection). The Gnostic is portrayed as one who does good for the selfish motive of perfection and not for the sake of the Good itself. Clement defines true perfection as knowing and loving God.

5   Clement considers faith and hope which do not exclude the intellect. Divine things are concealed in symbols to train the believer. The more profound matters of God are expressed symbolically in Scripture since they are reserved for mature Christians striving for perfection. The sacrifice acceptable to God is abstraction from the mundane matters of life and passions. Ultimately, God cannot be understood except by a gift of revelation. The Greeks derived opinions of God from the Hebrews (who were the recipients of revelation).

6   The true philosopher alone is pious. The Greeks, having gained their knowledge of divine matters secondhand, had some knowledge of God but do not possess true philosophy. Knowledge is desirable for its own sake and not merely out of a desire for personal perfection. Philosophy serves this goal and is thus useful. Clement examines Gnostic doctrines of the Decalogue.

7   The Christian has a true *gnosis* and is unjustly condemned by the Greeks as an atheist in that knowledge of God is gained through Christ. Christian prayers are presented as superior to pagan sacrifices. The Christian Gnostic (i.e., the true philosopher as opposed to the heretical gnostic) is so predisposed to the truth that an oath is not necessary. This knowledge of God leads to perfection. Clement describes the Church before the advent of heresies.

8   Clement considers that demonstration, i.e., discourse which by means of reason leads to truth, is necessary to gain knowledge although all philosophers admit that the first principles are not demonstrable but must be accepted *a priori*. Clement considers how things are classified and named, then considers causation.

Clement's use of non-Christian authors is impressive. In the *Miscellanies*, he has a particular affinity for Plato, Hesiod, Euripides and Menander as well as material from Plutarch, Empedocles, Orpheus, Sophocles and Solon. It is apparent that Clement possessed a wide knowledge of Hellenistic and Latin literature. Unlike other authors, such as Minucius Felix, who obviously consulted a compendium of philosophical opinions, Clement's citations and allusions are so extensive and explicit as to imply first-hand knowledge of his sources. Regarding these philosophers and poets whom Clement cites, he holds that "there always was . . . a natural revelation of the one almighty God amongst all right-thinking men, most of whom retaining some respect for truth, apprehended the eternal goodness in the providence of God . . . ."[3] The philosophy of the Greeks was preparatory to what would be fully revealed in Christ. Christ, therefore, revealed the true philosophy and Christianity is the perfected philosophy. At this point he is in agreement with Justin. To Clement, philosophy as practiced by Greeks and Romans is a mixture of good and bad thinking. In *Str.* 1.7, Clement advocates an eclectic approach to philosophy in which the Christian, having been enlightened by Christ, is to distinguish between that which is from God and that which belongs to the vain inventions of humankind. Clement understands "righteousness" to include the idea of "right-knowing." Since philosophy contains vain elements, which for Clement are those of human derivation as opposed to those divinely inspired, he can be found denigrating philosophy as well as employing it. We find him rejecting, for example, sophistry whose purpose is to make false opinion sound like the truth (*Str.* 1.8), Epicureanism which deifies the senses (1.11), and Stoicism which asserts the presence of the deity in all matter (1.11). Clement sees these false philosophies as the vain deceits villified by Paul in Colossians 2 (1.11). Therefore, the reader must take care not to read a total rejection of the philosopher's task into critical remarks on any given aspect of philosophy. If Clement, by his extensive citation of Greek and Latin literature, appears overly pedantic, he is simply engaging in the custom of his age, as Chadwick pointed out:

> If he [Clement] drags in anecdotes and scraps of scholarly erudition in a
> faintly pedantic manner, we may find the same manner . . . in writers of

---

[3] H. B. Timothy, *The Early Christian Apologists and Greek Philosophy Exemplified by Irenaeus, Tertullian and Clement of Alexandria* (Assen, 1973), 63. Timothy is making reference to *Str.* 5.13. 87.2.

his time like Aelian, or in those donnish sages who converse over imaginary dinners in the pages of Athenaeus. Clement and they belong equally to an intellectual society where philosophical speculation is moving almost wholly within a framework of ideas laid down by Greek philosophers five or six hundred years previously, with the natural consequence that philosophy has become scholasticism and the instinct for scholarship has turned to an antiquarian passion for amassing facts.[4]

Clement, therefore, was a product of his age and, unlike many of his fellow Christian writers, was quite well read. His acquaintance with both Greek and Latin literature was extensive and his literary style reflected the pedantic antiquarianism of his day. Clement reflects a genuine cultural fusion of Hellenism with Christianity. This stands in contrast with Minucius Felix whose rhetorical skill in the *Octavius,* itself a product of Latin culture, is used for the vilification of that same culture.

Chronography and Josephus

Clement had a particular interest in chronography. In the *Stromata* we discover the typical Christian concern to demonstrate the antiquity of Judaism in order to maintain the dependence of Greek philosophy upon Jewish Law. *Str.* 1.21 makes it clear that "the philosophy according to the Hebrews"[5] was the most ancient of philosophies and the precursor of Greek thought (1.21 [101, 1]). Clement points to the works of Tatian, Cassian, and even Apion as evidence for the antiquity of Moses and the Hebrews.

Clement's approach is not to compare biblical concepts with those of Greek philosophy but to parallel events of biblical history with events of Greek myth and history. He cites comments of Acusilaus, Apollodorus, Aegius, Dercylus, Hesiod, Heraclides of Pontus, Philocorus, Archimachus, Onomacritus, Alexander Polyhistor, Demetrius (the author of *On the Kings in Judea*), Eupolemos, and Plato. Clement seeks to prove that the Mosaic period antedated even the Trojan war. There is nothing novel about this except that Clement meticulously parallels biblical and Greek history. The author is not merely concerned with demonstrating the antiquity of Hebrew vis-à-vis Greek culture but is also interested in fixing the actual dates of the major events recounted in the Bible. To do this he must parallel the events mentioned in the Bible with those of Greek history whose dates were more or less firmly established. Although the purpose of the chapter is to demonstrate the greater antiquity of the Hebrew, and by extension the Christian, tradition, most of the chapter is dedicated to a chronographical summary of biblical history. Although Julius Africanus

---

[4] Henry Chadwick, *Early Christian Thought and the Classical Tradition. Studies in Justin, Clement, and Origen* (New York, 1966), 36.

[5] ἡ κατὰ ʽΕβραίους φιλοσοφία

possesses the title of "Father of Christian Chronography," one can already see an interest in chronography in this somewhat earlier work.

Josephus appears in this chapter of the *Stromata* (1.21 [147, 2]) as Clement calculates the length of time from Moses to the tenth year of Antoninus:

> The Jew Flavius Josephus, who composed the history of the Jews, calculating the periods, wrote that from Moses to David there were 585 years, and from David to the second year of Vespasian 1,179 years. Then from that until the tenth year of Antonius 77 years. Thus from Moses to the tenth year of Antonius there are 1,831 years in all. (*Str.* 1.21 [147.2-3])[6]

Clement does not identify his literary source for these figures. However, the second number, 1179 years from David to the second year of Vespasian's reign, is an obvious reference to *B.J.* 6.435ff. Josephus there states that Jerusalem was captured by the Romans in the second year of Vespasian's reign (435) and that the period from David to the destruction of the Temple by Titus was 1179 years (439). However, the origin of the first number, 585 years from Moses to David, is more difficult to discover.[7] Josephus simply does not provide this number or any number of years for this period. Further, if one were to add the figures of the generations between Moses and David, one could not arrive at 585 years. There is no textual evidence for such a reading in the Josephan material but it is possible that Clement arrived at his 585-year period based on other numbers provided by Josephus. If Josephus did not mention the duration of the period from Moses to David, he did provide the number of years between the Exodus and the building of the Temple. *A.J.* 8. 61ff. informs the reader that from the Exodus to the building of the Temple were 592 years. From this figure it is possible that Clement calculated the 585 years from Moses to David. The same passage in *A.J.* 8 informs us that Solomon constructed the Temple in the fourth year of his reign. Subtracting these four years as well as the seventy years of David's life (*A.J.* 7.389; cf. I Kings 2:11 and II Samuel 5:5) and adding to this figure the 40 years from the Exodus back to Moses' birth yields a total of 558 years from the birth of Moses to that of David. Clement's reckoning, however, is not 558 but 585 years. There is no textual evidence to support a reading of 558 and a scribal transposition is unlikely given the dissimilarity between the characters used for 58 (νή) and 85 (πέ). The most likely explanation is a transposition of the two numbers (πεντήκοντα ὀκτώ into ὀγδοήκοντα πέντε) in the mind of Clement at the time of composition. Clement must have

---

[6] Φλαύιος δὲ ᾽Ιώσηπος ὁ ᾽Ιουδαῖος ὁ τὰς ᾽Ιουδαϊκὰς συντάξας ἱστορίας καταγαγὼν τοὺς χρόνους φησὶν ἀπὸ Μωυσέως ἕως Δαβὶδ ἔτη γίγνεσθαι φπέ, ἀπὸ δὲ Δαβὶδ ἕως Οὐσπεσιανοῦ δευτέρου ἔτους αρθ᾽. εἶτα ἀπὸ τούτου μέχρι ᾽Αντωνίνου δεκάτου ἔτους ἔτη οζ᾽, ὡς εἶναι ἀπὸ Μωυσέως ἐπὶ τὸ δέκατου ἔτος ᾽Αντωνίνου πάντα ἔτη αωλγ᾽.

[7] Clement could not be thinking of a biblical reference in that the Heb. and Luc. give a figure of 480 years and the LXX 440.

gotten his figure for the period from the Exodus to the Temple from *A.J.* 8, given that the other mention of this duration in the Josephan corpus (*C.A.* 2.19) reads 612 years.

A fragment of dubious origin purporting to be from Cyril of Alexandria against the emperor Julian states that Clement made use of a work by Sanchoniathon translated into Greek by Josephus.[8] The Phoenician Sagchoniathon (or Sanchuniathon), according to Philon of Byblos (64-c. 140 C.E.), composed a history of Phoenician religious rites and demonstrated the antiquity of the Trojan war. Philon's testimony is extant only in Eusebius (*P.E.* 1.9-10 and 4.16). Philon claimed to have utilized Sanchuniathon's work in his own studies of Phoenician religion. Of course, one cannot insist upon the accuracy of Philon's claims as transmitted by Eusebius. However, they appear more plausible than the opinion of the fragment relating to Clement, given Philon's work in history and language as attested in other sources.

Summary

Clement cites the *Jewish War* and the *Antiquities of the Jews* as proof that ancient historians demonstrate the considerable antiquity of the Jewish people and the precedence of Moses vis-à-vis the Greek philosophers who borrowed from his philosophy. We shall see this same theme expanded by Eusebius who, following *Against Apion*, presents Moses as a philosopher without peer. Further, Clement's interest in chronology presages the more extensive treatment by Julius the African to whom we turn next.

---

[8] Fragment nr. 51 in O. Stählin, ed., *Clemens Alexandrinus. Dritter Band. Stromata Buch VII und VIII. Excerpta ex Theodoto–Eclogai Propheticae Quis Dives Salvetur– Fragmente,* GCS 17 (Leipzig, 1909), 225. The fragment can be also found in PG 76:813.

Chapter Six

Julius Africanus

Socrates (Socrates, *H.E.* 2.35) attests to the standing of Julius Africanus as one of the three great Alexandrian theologians along with Clement and Origen. Eusebius informs us that Julius came to Alexandria to study under Heraclas (Eusebius, *H.E.* 6.31) who had succeeded Origen as head of the Alexandrian School (*H.E.* 6.26). As to Julius' writings, Eusebius mentions the African, "the author of the books entitled *Kestoí*",[1] and "the five books of *Chronographies*"[2] (*H.E.* 6.31). In the same passage Eusebius also refers to two letters: one written to Origen regarding the African's uncertainty over whether the Susanna story in Daniel was authentic or a forgery and the second addressed to Aristides regarding the genealogies in Matthew and Luke. Fragments of these documents may be found in works by Eusebius, Suidas, Syncellus, and Photius. The letter to Origen may be found in Origen's works. The preface to a spurious work on events occurring in Persia at the time of Christ's birth claims authorship by Africanus. The introduction in Migne (PG 10:97-98) to this piece admonishes the reader as to the superstitious nature of the work and rejects the attribution to Africanus. There is one further document of questionable origin attributed to Africanus, the *Acts of Symphorosa and Her Seven Sons*. This brief manuscript claims authorship by the African; however, there is no ancient attestation of his having recounted the martyrdom of these eight saints.

The *Kestoí* has also aroused some suspicion as to its origins. Although its authorship by Julius Africanus is confirmed by ancient authors, doubts about the *Kestoí* were raised by some scholars in the last century owing to the author's interest in magic and sorcery.[3] Suidas, in the *Index Scriptorum*, informs us that the *Kestoí* were written by "Africanus, Sextus, the African philosopher."[4] This

---

[1] ὁ τῶν ἐπιγεγραμμένων Κεστῶν συγγραφεὺς ἐγνωρίζετο. Κεστοί, literally "embroidered girdles," indicates the varied nature of the work. Compare this to Clement's Strwmatei'" *(Miscellanies)*.

[2] τὸν ἀριθμὸν πέντε Χρονογραφιῶν

[3] H. Gelzer, *Sextus Julius Africanus und die byzantinische Chronographie* (Leipzig, 1885; rpt. New York, 1967), 1:2f. Gelzer provides a bibliography of writers on both sides of the argument.

[4] PG 117:1218: "Africanus, Sextus, Afer philosophus, qui scripsit Kestou;", *Cestos . . .*"

Sextus Africanus is identified as the friend of Origen. Those who deny that Julius Africanus wrote the *Kestoí* postulate that the Sextus Africanus of Suidas is a different Africanus and the attribution in Eusebius' *H.E.* 6.31 is an interpolation made before Syncellus and Photius read Eusebius and Suidas in the ninth century. As there is no textual evidence for these assertions, the denial that Julius Africanus, the author of the *Chronography*, wrote the *Kestoí* is based on the argument that this great Alexandrian could not have written such a superstitious work. This particular problem, however, does not relate directly to our inquiries.

It is impossible to determine the identity of all the sources utilized by Julius Africanus, including those for the five-volume *Chronography*, which is of special interest to us. The *Chronography* relates events from the Creation to Elagabalus in the first quarter of the third century C.E.[5] The extant fragments include material on the chronography of Genesis, parallels between the biblical history from Abraham to Moses and the Olympiads, and an interpretation of the seventy weeks of Daniel. We also find a history of the late Hasmonean and Herodian periods. Africanus reckons the time span from various events of Old Testament history to the period of Christ. The fragments we find reflect the interests of those who are transmitters of the *Chronography*, which may be somewhat different from Africanus' own emphases. Additionally problematic is our discovery that Africanus is summarized rather than quoted. With regard to Africanus' use of Josephan material, we cannot know when Julius Africanus might be quoting Josephus or merely summarizing him. Therefore, we can say little about the text of Josephus utilized by Julius Africanus.

Our fragments indicate that, like Clement of Alexandria (see *Str.* 1.21), Julius Africanus is interested in portraying the biblical period against the backdrop of world history. Africanus is writing to a Christian audience which is more knowledgeable regarding Greek mythology and history than events described in the Bible. Africanus' use of the Olympiads to date biblical history reflects his own cultural affinities as well as those of his audience.

Josephan Material in Julius Africanus

Although it is certain that Julius Africanus made use of Josephan material, we may also be sure that he was not totally dependent on Josephus. While we shall discover that the *Chronography* utilized Josephan material for the period from Alexander to Herod, Africanus' *Letter to Aristides* (PG 10:51-64) cites an alternative tradition regarding the origins of Herod's family which cannot be

---

[5]Gelzer, 1:28-29. Gelzer has reconstructed a plausible table of contents from the extant fragments: Book 1: from the Creation to the Flood. Book 2: to Moses. Book 3: from Moses to the time of the first Olympiad (which Africanus identified as contemporary with Ahaz). Book 4: to the fall of Persia. Book 5: from Alexander to Elagabalus.

found in Josephus or any other extant source. While part four of the letter (PG 10:59-60)[6] contains a tradition regarding Herod's father, Antipater, whose father, named Herod, is said to have been a priest in a temple of Apollo, Josephus informs us that Antipater's father was the Idumean Antipater who was prefect of that province at the appointment of the Hasmonean Alexander (*A.J.* 14.9-10). Africanus closes with the statement that "these things can be found as well in the Greek histories."[7] Which "Greek histories" remains a mystery.

Although Africanus' *Chronography* is not extant, Syncellus made use of the *Chronography* in his own chronography for the period of Jewish history from Alexander to Seleucus Philopater (i.e., until the eve of the Maccabean Revolt). The material borrowed from the African included material drawn from the *Antiquities of the Jews* 12. Syncellus is probably paraphrasing Africanus in that he feels free to introduce comments based on the chronography of Panadorus (which dates from the early fifth century) into the narrative borrowed from Africanus and thus we may not draw any conclusions as to the nature of the Josephan text read by Africanus.

The Josephan material from *A.J.* 12 employed in our fragments from the *Chronography* concerns the fate of Jerusalem after Alexander and the Tobiad romance. Gelzer[8] identified the Josephan passages in the fragments although their locations are not all correctly assigned. The references of the fragments of the *Chronography* in Dindorf's edition of Syncellus and the correct Josephan passages used follow:

Syncellus	A.J. 12	Subject
512.8-10	43	Simon the Just
512.19-22	158-160	Onias and Joseph the Tobiad
515.18-20	4	Ptolemy Soter seizes Jerusalem
520.10-11	119	Seleucus Nicator grants Jews citizenship in Asia and Syria
537.1-2	131	Antiochus annexes Judea
537.7-10	154	Antiochus gives daughter Cleopatra to Ptolemy with Coela-Syria, Samaria, and Judea as dowry
537.11-12	131	Ptolemy sends Scopas to capture Coele-Syria but is defeated by Antiochus

[6]Reference to this tradition may be found by Syncellus in G. Dindorf, ed., *Georgias Syncellus et Nicephorus CP, Corpus Scriptorum Historiae Byzantinae* 21, ed. B. G. Niebuhr (Bonn, 1829), 1:561.11ff.

[7]Ταῦτα μὲν δὴ κοινὰ καὶ ταῖς Ἑλλήνων ἱστορίαις.

[8]Gelzer, 1:246-265.

Syncellus	A.J. 12	Subject
537.12-14	132-133	The Jews demonstrate support for Antiochus
537.14-15	134	Antiochus decides to reward Jews for their support
537.16-18	196-222	Hyrcanus the Tobiad
	228-236	

Although we cannot assert that Josephus was Africanus' sole source for Jewish history from Alexander to Herod, *Antiquities* 12 was a major source for this period. It is to be noted that fragments from the African's works dealing with other periods of history do not demonstrate the same level of dependence on Josephan material. Julius Africanus deemed Josephus an authority on this period of history and drew from the *Antiquities*. Unfortunately, we cannot say to what extent Africanus drew from Josephus elsewhere, if indeed he did at all. What can be said is that Julius Africanus' interest in chronography had its roots in the work of the earlier Alexandrian theologian, Clement of Alexandria. Like Clement, Africanus demonstrates the considerable antiquity of the Jews whose heir is the Church. However, as Gelzer has pointed out, the African did not do so by stressing the philosophical dependence of the Greeks upon Moses but saw the fixing of events in the life of Israel in a chronological framework as an end in itself *(Selbstzweck)*.[9] Gelzer errs, however, in drawing too sharp a distinction between Clement's and Africanus' purposes. In the *Miscellanies,* Clement presented the thesis that the Mosaic system not only antedated Greek philosophy but that Hellenistic thought was dependent on the philosopher Moses. The chronography of the African complements and expands upon Clement's evidence for this thesis: Julius provides a complete chronographic history of Moses and the Jews whose origins stretch back into distant antiquity. Julius Africanus' purpose depends upon the work of Clement who provided the philosophical justification for the African's chronographic labors.

---

[9]Gelzer, 1:23.

Chapter Seven

Pseudo-Justin

The *Exhortation to the Greeks* (ΛΟΓΟΣ ΠΑΡΑΙΝΕΤΙΚΟΣ ΠΡΟΣ ΕΛΛΗΝΑΣ or *Cohortatio ad Graecos*) is a product of unknown authorship and uncertain origin. It is an attempt to demonstrate Hellenism's failure to lead to true religion and to attain the truth arrived at by Christianity. Pseudo-Justin does this without resorting to Scripture as proof of Christianity's claims to be the one true faith. Rather, to prove his claims he relies upon the antiquity of Moses, as attested to by literary authorities, and the absence of a consensus among Greek poets and philosophers on religion. We see this element in Julius Africanus, who may have some connection to this work, and Eusebius. Josephus' role in the *Exhortation* is minor, being confined to a list of recognized historians who have recorded biographical details of Moses.

Chapter(s):

1	The author explains that he seeks to demonstrate the fallaciousness of Greek religion and the truth of Christianity.
2	The poets are unfit teachers for their opinions are ludicrous.
3-7	The poets and philosophers cannot agree and are inconsistent in their opinions on religion and the nature of the universe.
8	This is to be contrasted with the antiquity, inspiration, and harmony among Christian teachers.
9-12	The antiquity, wisdom, and reliability of Moses are superior to that of the Greek authorities.
13	The biblical tradition is trustworthy owing to its careful preservation.
14	The Greeks are warned of the coming judgment.
15-24	Allusions to monotheism can be discovered in the writings of Greek poets and philosophers.
25-34	Plato is shown to be dependent upon Scripture for certain significant ideas.

35-36   The author appeals to the Greeks to accept Christianity for the Greek writers are uninspired by the Holy Spirit and are thus ignorant.

37   The prophecies of the Sibyl support biblical claims.

38   The author makes a final appeal to his readers to accept the Christian teaching, for it is the truth.

Dating of the *Exhortation to the Greeks*

The earliest attribution of the *Exhortation* to Justin seems to be by John of Damascus. Harnack noted a citation from the fifth chapter of the *Exhortation* in the Codex Rupef. with the superscription, τοῦ ἀγ.'Ιουστίου τοῦ φιλ. μαρτ. ἐκ τοῦ πρὸς "Ελληνας παραινετικοῦ.[1] Harnack further discovered a citation by Photius from Stephan Gobarus of what can be recognized as derivative from chapter 23 of the *Exhortation*. The citation from Gobarus, although not noting the actual source, attributes the passage to Pseudo-Justin. Thus the *Exhortation* can be linked with Pseudo-Justin no earlier than the sixth or seventh century given a traditional dating for Stephan Gobarus.[2]

Determining both the *terminus a quo* and the *terminus ad quem* poses considerable problems. It has been long recognized that the *Exhortation to the Greeks* does not belong within the Justinian corpus and yet an accurate determination of its origin is elusive. There is considerable difference between the literary styles of Justin and the author of this text.[3] That the *Exhortation to the Greeks* is not Justinian is evident in the author's attitude toward Greek philosophy. The *Exhortation* treats philosophy as a false science which fails both to elicit a consensus among its adherents and to lead to the truth. However, for the author of the authentic first *Apology*, the philosophy of the Greeks is not inconsistent with the Christian Gospel. Indeed, Justin invites Antoninus Pius to inspect the Christian faith and subject it to the rigors of philosophical inquiry (*Apology* 1.3). Justin does not see Christianity as the adversary of philosophy but as its fulfillment. In the *Dialogue with Trypho the Jew* we find him recognized as the philosopher (chapter 1). Justin seeks to make Christianity credible to the philosopher while the *Exhortation to the Greeks* dismisses philosophy as incredible.

Considerable verbal similarity exists between the ninth chapter of the *Exhortation* and the writing of Julius Africanus as he is cited by Eusebius (*P.E.* 10.10). Further, both the author of the *Exhortation* and Julius Africanus list a

---

[1] "from the Exhortation to the Greeks of Saint Justin, philospher and martyr"

[2] A. Harnack, "Die Überlieferung der griechischen Apologeten des 2. Jahrhunderts in der alten Kirche und im Mittelalter," in TU (Leipzig, 1883), 1:156-157.

[3] O. Bardenhewer, *Geschichte der altchristlichen Literatur* (Freiburg, 1902), 1:215.

number of historians who treated the subject of Moses (brackets indicate that the name is not to be found in the other's list):

Julius Africanus	Exhortation
Ogyges	Ogyges
Hellanicus	[Inachus]
Philocoros	Polemon
Castor	Hellanicus
Thallus	Philocorus
Diodorus	Castor
Alexander Polyhistor	Thallus
Polemon	Alexander Polyhistor
Apion son of Poseidonius	[Philo]
[Herodotus]	[Josephus]
Ptolemaeus of Mendes	Diodorus

It is noteworthy that in both lists Hellanicus and Philochorus are connected by an "and" as are Castor and Thallus. Schürer deemed Julius Africanus to be the primary source because he transmitted the story recorded in *Aristeas* regarding the composition of the LXX in which the seventy translators together produced a Greek translation of the Hebrew Bible for King Ptolemy.[4] The *Exhortation*, however, transmits the more fanciful tale of the seventy working independently and yet producing identical translations. For Schürer, since the latter story gained in popularity over the years, it is more probable that the author of the *Exhortation* was dependent upon Julius Africanus than the reverse. However, the fact that the story of the seventy independent and yet identical translations of the Hebrew Bible is as early as Philo militates against Schürer's argument.

---

[4]E. Schürer, "Julius Africanus als Quelle der Pseudo-Justin'schen Cohortatio ad Graecos," *ZKG* 2 (1877-78), 319-331.

Völter,[5] Asmus,[6] and Dräseke[7] agreed with Schürer that Julius Africanus antedated the author of the *Exhortation to the Greeks*. However, Völter in particular improved upon Schürer's thesis by noting that, while Julius Africanus provides details about each historian in his list, the author of the *Exhortation*, being interested only in who treated the subject of Moses and not in chronography, summarized Julius' material. This seems more likely to Völter than Julius Africanus' borrowing a general outline from the *Exhortation to the Greeks* and then expanding it. Völter recognizes the tentativeness of his own argument for he allows that both authors could have depended on a common source. However, Völter, Asmus and Dräseke each advance the theory that the *Exhortation* was a response to Julian's edict (362 C.E.) written by the Syrian author Apollinaris. Our knowledge of Julian's edict which restored Hellenistic religion to its former supremacy and removed Christians from the academies and public offices comes from Sozomen's *Ecclesiastical History* 5 (PG 67:1269-1272). Sozomen recounts that Apollinarius, a Syrian and contemporary of Basil and Gregory, wrote a apology of the Christian faith entitled *On Truth* (Περὶ Ἀλγθείας) in which he sought to demonstrate, without appealing to Scripture, that the philosophers were far from the "true" religion. Further, Apollinarus wrote a history of the Old Testament as far back as Saul in epic style as a replacement for Homer. Apollinarius was knowledgeable in Greek literature as well as being a competent philosopher. The author of the *Exhortation* was knowledgeable in hellenistic philosophy and took great pains to demonstrate the unreliability of Plato of whom Julian was especially fond. The author of the *Exhortation* makes much use of Homer and we know from Sozomen that Apolinarius wrote a biblical replacement. Therefore, the three German scholars propose that our *Exhortation to the Greeks* is none other than the lost *On Truth* which was composed sometime in the seventh decade of the fourth century C.E.

The preceding theory may be plausible but all that may be safely said about the *Exhortation to the Greeks* is that it is not Justinian but was probably composed sometime in the third century C.E. (in the latter half if the author read Julius Africanus) or soon after Julian's edict in the fourth century. The tone of the work implies that Christianity has not defeated Hellenism; the work seems to be an attack on the *status quo*. The author confines himself to Jewish Scripture while avoiding the New Testament. This factor reflects Pseudo-Justin's concern with the antiquity of Moses and the Hebrews; nothing more can

---

[5]D. Völter, "Über Zeit und Verfasser des pseudo-justinischen Cohortatio ad Graecos," *ZWT* 26 (1883), 180-215.

[6]J. R. Asmus, "Ist die pseudojustinische Cohortatio ad Graecos eine Streitschrift gegen Julian?," *ZWT* 38 (1895), 115-155; "Eine Encyklika Julians des Abtrünnigen und ihre Vorläufler," *ZKG* 16 (1895-96), 45-71 and 220-252; and "Ein Bindeglied zwischen des pseudojustinischen Cohortatio ad Graecos und Julians Polemik gegen die Galiläer," *ZWT* 40 (1897), 268-284.

[7]J. Dräseke, "Der Vefasser des fälschlich Justinus beigelegten ΛΟΓΟΣ ΠΑΡΑΙΝΕΤΙΚΟΣ ΠΡΟΣ ΕΛΛΗΝΑΣ," *ZKG* 7 (1884-85), 257-302.

be construed from it. There is no exultation in the triumph of biblical prophecy nor has philosophy been appropriated by the Church as occurred after its political victory in the fourth century.

Greek religion according to Pseudo-Justin

Pseudo-Justin seeks to demonstrate the superiority of Christian teaching by illustrating the weakness of the Hellenistic religious system. In particular, he inveighs against the teachers of religion (qeosebeivaß didaskavlouß) on whose credibility, according to Pseudo-Justin, the Greek religion rests:

> It seems good to me, first to examine both our and your teachers of religion, who they were and how great they were, and in what times they lived so that those who have received the false religion from their predecessors, now perceiving, may be set free from that ancient error. And that we may distinctly and manifestly prove that we follow the religion of our predecessors according to God.[8] (PG 6:241)

In his diatribe Pseudo-Justin attacks the two groups which represent the Hellenistic system: the poets and the philosophers. Homer is singled out as the chief of the poets whose work, particularly the *Iliad,* is treated as exemplary. To Pseudo-Justin, the works of the poets constitute a ridiculous theogony which can be dismissed for reasons he deems self-evident (chapter 2): (1) The gods are born of water; (2) Zeus provides humanity with the tragedy of war; (3) the gods conspire against each other; (4) the gods even suffer at the hands of humans. It should be noted that Pseudo-Justin's criticisms of the religious tradition represented by Homer are shared by philosophers such as the Stoics. Nevertheless, for Pseudo-Justin, Homer's depiction of the gods allows the Greek the choice of accepting a ridiculous portrait of the pantheon or rejecting the existence of the gods altogether. Pseudo-Justin's diatribe appears to be directed at those Greeks who have moved beyond the primitive mythology of the Homeric epics but for whom the antiquity and literary preeminence of Homer nevertheless retained importance. Pseudo-Justin rejects this later attraction as the Homeric epic allows for no other image of the deities except that of a petulant and and compassionless pantheon. Homer's gods neither inspire the noble aims of many Greeks nor do they constitute objects of worship. For Pseudo-Justin, one must either accept Homer's gods wholeheartedly or utterly reject them.

After dismissing Greek poetry as a potential source for a beneficent religion, Pseudo-Justin turns to the philosophers. His tactic is one of pointing out both the disagreements among the Greek philosophers and even internal disagreements

---

[8]ἔδοξέ μοι καλῶς ἔχειν, πρῶτον μὲν τοὺς τῆς θεοσεβεῖς ἡμῶν τε καὶ ὑμῶν ἐξετάσαι διδασκάλους, οἵ τινες καὶ ὅσοι, καὶ καθ᾽ οὓς γεγόνασι χρόνους· ἵν᾽ οἱ μὲν πρότεπο τὴν ψευδώνυμον θεοσέβειαν παρὰ τῶν προγόνω παρειληφότες, νῦν γοῦν αἰσθόμενοι, τῆς παλαιᾶς ἐκείνας ἀπαλλαγῶσι πλάνης· ἡμεῖς δὲ, σαφῶς καὶ φανερῶς ἡμᾶς αὐτοὺς ἀποδείξωμεν τῇ τῶν κατὰ θεὸν προγόνων ἑπομένους θεοσεβείᾳ.

within their works by contrast with the harmony of the Scriptures and among Christian teachers.

Pseudo-Justin turns his attention first to the School of Thales, not citing the literature of this school as he does for Homer but merely summarizing the positions. He recognizes, that for many Greeks, the wisdom of the philosophers is more attractive than the mythology of Homer:

> And if you beg off citing the poets because you say it is permitted them to fashion myths and to relate many things about the gods far from the truth, do you think to have others for your teachers of religion, or how do you say they learned it [i.e., religion] themselves? For it is impossible to know about great and divine matters without having first acquired learning from the initiated. You will doubtless say the sages and philosophers. For to them you will flee as to a fortified wall whenever someone quotes opinions of the poets regarding the gods.[9] (PG 6:245-247)

Pseudo-Justin considers disagreements over the identity of the first principle of all things which Thales identified as water, Anaximander as the Infinite and Anaximenes as air. In noting that all three philosophers were from Miletus, Pseudo-Justin emphasizes the confusion which reigned even in this one circle of scholars. He continues by citing opinions from Heraclitus and Hippasus from Metapontus, Anaxagoras of Clazomeme, and Archelaus, the son of Apollodorus, who all belong to the School of Thales and none of whom agree on this fundamental principle of natural philosophy.

Pseudo-Justin points out that beyond the Thalesian school there is still no agreement on the first principle. Pythagoras identifies the first principle as number. Epicurus maintains that the first principles of all things are "bodies perceptible by reason, not admitting the void."[10] These are the philosophers to whom, as Pseudo-Justin wryly observes, the Greeks look for knowledge of true religion but whose opinions are irreconcilable.

Pseudo-Justin then turns his attention to the two leading Greek philosophers, Plato and Aristotle. He seldom cites any material from Plato[11] and never quotes from the Aristotelian corpus. Rather, he summarizes the

---

[9]Εἰ δὲ τοὺς ποιητὰς παραιτεῖσθε λέγειν, ἐπειδὴ μύθους τε αὐτοῖς πλάττειν ἐξεῖναι φατε, καὶ πολλὰ πόρρω τῆς ἀληθείας περὶ θεῶν μυθωδῶς διεξιέαι, τίνας ἑτέρους τῆς θεοσεβείας ὑμῶν διδασκάλους ἔχειν οἴσθε, ἢ πῶς ταύτην αὐτοὺς μεμαθηκέναι φατὲ ἀδύνατον γὰρ τοὺς μὴ πρότερον παρὰ τῶν εἰδότων μεμαθηκότας τὰ οὕτω μεγάλα καὶ θεῖα πράγματα γινώσκειν. Τοὺς σοφοὺς πάντως δήπου καὶ φιλοσόφους λέξετε · ἐπὶ τούτους γάρ, ὥσπερ ἐπὶ τεῖχος ὀχυρόν, καταφεύγειν, ἐπειδάν τισ ὑμῖν τὰς τῶν τοιητῶν περὶ θεῶν ἀπαγγέλλῃ δόξας.

[10]σώματα λόγῳ θεωρητα . . . ἀμέτοχα κενοῦ. These primordial bodies are different in nature from the void in which they exist.

[11]The *Republic* is cited in chapters 5 and 26. The *Timaeus* appears only in chapter 26.

positions of these philosophers. That these are "thought to be the most renowned and accomplished philosophers among them" [12] (PG 6:249) accounts for Platonic ideas being treated in fifteen out of thirty-eight chapters.

Pseudo-Justin seeks to demonstrate, as he did with the School of Thales, the ignorance of Plato and Aristotle by emphasizing contrary opinions. In chapters 5 and 6 Pseudo-Justin highlights disagreements over the nature of God, the number of first principles, and the nature of the human soul. Further, in chapter 7 we find that internal inconsistencies can be found within Plato, the master philosopher. Pseudo-Justin notes that Plato declares there to be three first principles of the universe, God, matter and form; however, elsewhere the philosopher adds the universal soul as a fourth principle (PG 6:256). Further, Plato is at odds with himself over whether creation is liable to destruction or if certain created things are indestructible. Therefore, Plato and all the philosophers stand convicted of ignorance by their own contradictory testimony. For all his criticisms of Greek thought, Pseudo-Justin here employs the common rhetorical device of attacking the internal inconsistencies of one's opponents. Pseudo-Justin is never more hellenistic than in his diatribe against Hellenism.

Although Pseudo-Justin rejects the witness of both the Greek poets and philosophers, he does not hesitate to appeal to them when it serves his purpose. If the Greeks do not serve as sources for knowledge of true religion, nevertheless some are presented as crypto-monotheists. In chapter 15 we discover a citation from Orpheus to Musaeus, whom Orpheus instructs: "Look to the one, universal king; one, self-begotten, alone, from whom all things are sprung." [13] (PG 6:269)

Even the Sibyl (chapter 16), recognized as a prophetess by such eminent minds as Plato and Aristophanes, declares, "There is one God alone who is omnipotent, unbegotten."[14] (PG 6:272)

Pseudo-Justin notes (chap. 17) that even Homer alludes to monotheism. Although not able to recall the exact citation (it is the *Iliad* 9.445), Pseudo-Justin notes that the Phoenix uses the singular when speaking to Achilles of the deity. Further, Pseudo-Justin finds Odysseus (*Iliad* 2.206) affirming the virtue of monotheistic rule.

Sophocles (chapter 18) provides not merely testimony to the existence of the single deity but condemns idolatry:

> In truth there is one God, who made heaven and the broad earth, and the bright waves of the sea, the strong winds. Many of us mortals err in heart; being distressed we set up images of the gods out of stone and

---

[12] ἀλλὰ παρὰ τῶν ἐδοξοτάτων καὶ τελειοτάτων ἐν ἀρετῇ νομισθέντων εἶναι παρ' αὐτοῖς φιλοσόφων .

[13] 'Ατραπιτοῦ, μοῦνον δ' ἐσόρα κόσμοιο ἄακτα. Εἶς ἐστ' αὐγενὴς · ἑνὸς ἔκγονα πάντα τέτυκται

[14] Εἶς θεὸς ὃς μονος ἐστὶν ὑπερμεγέθης, ἀγένητος.

wood, or figures of gold or ivory as a solace. We offer sacrifices and beautiful rites; thus we think we perform a pious work.[15] (PG 6:273, 276)

Pythagoras (chap. 19) is construed as a monotheist owing to his concept of the unity of God. Pseudo-Justin delights to point out that Pythagoras had moved to the point of describing God as the "first of all things, the light of heaven, and the father of all things"[16] (PG 6:276).

Plato is deemed to have come to an acceptance of monotheism during a sojourn in Egypt (chapter 20) but to have declined to make his views widely known because of concern for his safety (chapters 21 and 23). Pseudo-Justin likens 'Εγώ, εἰμι ὁ ὤν[17] of the LXX to Plato's ὄτος, his concept of "Being" (PG 6:280). Although Pseudo-Justin has discredited Plato as a knowledgeable source for religious matters, he can nevertheless find a use for the philosopher. Plato is seen as being indebted to the prophets (chapter 26) for knowledge of the resurrection (chapter 27). Plato is even presented as having been familiar with the Pentateuch from which he developed his concept of form as the third principle of matter (chapter 29). In that Plato allegedly read Exodus 25:9 (in which Moses is to build the Tabernacle according to the pattern God would reveal), the philosopher incorrectly assumed that the pattern or form possesses a separate existence from matter. Further, Pseudo-Justin posits that Plato developed his notion that time was created along with the heavens from Genesis 1 in that the heavens were created on the first day (chapter 33). Therefore, both time and the heavens share a common point of origin.

Pseudo-Justin also finds indications in the Homeric literature (chapters 28 and 30) that the Pentateuch was known and utilized in the composition of the *Iliad* and the *Odyssey*. Even the oracles of the Sibyl are likened to the utterances of the biblical prophets (chapter 37).

Pseudo-Justin's treatment of the Greek poets and philosophers is thus bifurcated. He first seeks to discredit the authorities of Greek culture and religion by citing inconsistencies among them and within themselves. Yet he maintains that the eminent literary and philosophical minds of the Greeks were dependent upon Moses and the Bible. To do this Pseudo-Justin must first demonstrate the antiquity of Moses.

---

[15]Εἰς ταῖς ἀληθείαισιν, εἷς ἐστιν θεὸς, 'Ος οὐρανὸν τέτευχε, καὶ γαῖαν μακρὰν, Πόντου τε χαροπὸν οἶδμα, κανέμων βίας. θνητοὶ δὲ πολλοὶ καρδίᾳ πλανώμενοι, 'Ιδρυσάμεσθα πημάτων παράψυχὴν θεῶν ἀγάλματ' ἐκ λίθων τε καὶ ξύλων, "Η χρυσοτεύκτων ἢ ἐλεφαντίνων τύπους' θυσίας τε τούτοις καὶ καλὰς πανηγύρεις Τεύχοντες, οὕτως εὐσεθεῖν νομίζομεν. The citation is from Pseudo-Sophocles; see PG 6:274n.

[16]ἀρχὰ πάντων, ἐν οὐρανῷ φωστὴρ, καὶ πάντων Πατὴρ.

[17]Exodus 4:14: I am who I am.

The Antiquity of Moses and the Witness of Philo and Josephus

Pseudo-Justin attaches particular importance to the antiquity of Moses. As Moses was recognized as being the primary prophet and lawgiver, to demonstrate his antiquity is to demonstrate the antiquity of not only the Jewish faith and the Bible but also that of the Church in that the "wisdom" of Moses and the prophet is seen as resident in Christianity. Pseudo-Justin is heir to the tradition of apologists going back to the Hellenistic historian Hecataeus of Abdera (fourth century B.C.E.) which depicts Moses as a wise-man and philosopher.[18] Like his Greco-Jewish predecessors, Pseudo-Justin seeks to demonstrate Moses' antiquity on the grounds that *antiquity confers authority:* Greater antiquity then betokens greater authority. To prove the superiority of Christianity over Greek philosophy, Pseudo-Justin must show that the roots of Christianity are more ancient than those of Greek religion and thought. It is necessary, therefore, to appeal to Jewish antiquity given that Christian antiquity apart from that of the mother religion is an impossibility.

In chapter 9, Pseudo-Justin arrays evidence for the antiquity of Moses. He cites the witness of Greek historians Polemon, Apion, Ptolemy the Mendesian, Hellanicus, Philochorus, Castor, Thallus and Alexander Polyhistor as to the prominence of Moses among the Jewish people. There is some incongruity in that Pseudo-Justin refers to Moses as "our" first prophet and religious teacher. However, it must be remembered that Pseudo-Justin assumes a continuity from Israel to the Church (the "true" Israel). Although Pseudo-Justin mentions the names of these historians, he does so merely to indicate that they were aware of Moses' significance in Jewish history. Evidence for Moses' antiquity is derived in part from Philo and Josephus. It is unclear to what extent Pseudo-Justin was acquainted with Josephus. Pseudo-Justin sees the significance of Josephus' witness in the very title of the work which contains his account of the life of Moses, the *Jewish Antiquities* ('Ιουδαϊκῆς 'Αρχαιολογίας in chapter 9; PG 6:257). Josephus' *Archaeology* redeems the Mosaic faith from obscurity by demonstrating its antiquity. Other than this, Josephus' significance is merely that Moses' life was narrated by him as well as by other prominent historians (chapters 10 and 13).

---

[18]B. Z. Wacholder, *Eupolemos. A Study of Judeo-Greek Literature* (Cincinnati, 1974), 85ff. Also, see J. G. Gager, *Moses in Greco-Roman Paganism* (Nashville, 1972), 25-37. Gager points out that the theme of Moses as wise-man may antedate Hecataeus given Pseudo-Justin's reference to Hellenicus (c. 500 B.C.E.).

As already established, Pseudo-Justin is concerned with demonstrating the bankruptcy of Greek thought by pointing out the internal contradictions in Greek philosophy and the riduculous image of the gods in Greek poetry. Further, Pseudo-Justin seeks to establish the greater antiquity of Moses and the Mosaic code which confers authority upon Israel (and the Church as the "true" Israel). There are interestingly similarities between the *Exhortation* and *Against Apion:* Greek culture and thought are not as ancient as that of the Jews, Greek philosophy is dependent upon Moses, and while one cannot turn to the Greeks for knowledge of true religion, they retain some truth from their contact with the Mosaic code. Nevertheless, Pseudo-Justin does not appear to have been influenced by this Josephan work. That Josephus demonstrated the antiquity of the Jews in his *Antiquities* is all that we can find in the *Exhortation*. Pseudo-Justin's argument may be based on a Christian *trope*. However, if we are to determine to what extent that *trope* was influenced by Josephus, we must look elsewhere.

Chapter Eight

Tertullian

Tertullian, born in Carthage c. 145 C.E. and died there c. 220, was a lawyer in Rome.[1] After returning from Rome to his native Carthage c. 195 C.E., he became a prolific writer, his best known work being the *Apology*. Eventually he allied himself with the Montanists and finally formed his own sect owing to what he viewed as lax discipline in the Church. His writing demonstrates considerable knowledge of Roman jurisprudence, rhetoric and literature.[2]

Eusebius informs us that Tertullian addressed an apology for Christianity to the Roman senate (*H.E.* 5.5.5). It is difficult to determine precisely where the *Apology* falls chronologically with respect to other works of Tertullian. Harnack dates the work c. 200 C.E., given that a Greek translation of the work was known in the early third century.[3]

The matter of the *Apology* is complicated by the nature of its relationship with the *Octavius* by Minucius Felix. As previously discussed, it is uncertain whether Minucius Felix made use of Tertullian's *Apology* or Tertullian read the *Octavius*.[4] In that the dating of the *Octavius* possesses its own difficulties, we are not aided in the matter of the *Apology*. The most that can be said is that the *Apology* was composed c. 200 C.E.

Chapter(s):

1-3   Tertullian deplores the misunderstanding and mistreatment of Christians at Roman hands.

4-6   Roman laws and society are decried as fallible and wicked.

7-9   Christians are falsely condemned of wickedness while their persecutors themselves are evil.

---

[1]Eusebius, *H.E.* 2.2.4 and Jerome, *Vir. Ill.* 53.

[2]See A. Harnack, *Geschichte der altchristlichen Litteratur bis Eusebius* (Leipzig, 1893), 2:667-687.

[3]Harnack, A. *Die griechische Übersetzung des Apologet. Tert.'s.* TU 8 (Leipzig, 1892), 4:4.

[4]See the chapter on Minucius Felix.

10-15	Roman deities are condemned as unworthy and based on mortals. Christians are made to suffer on account of these non-existent deities to whom even the Romans show disrespect.
16-17	Christians have been falsely accused of worshiping the head of an ass. However, they worship the one God.
18-20	God revealed Himself to the Jews and gave them writings of great antiquity. The antiquity of the Jews has been demonstrated. These sacred writings contain prophecies by which present misfortunes are interpreted and the future is assured.
21	Although Christ lived only recently, he too was a revelation of God.
22-24	The existence of spirits and angels points to the one God.
25-26	The Roman deities have not brought prosperity to Rome as Rome still suffers misfortunes. It is the one God who has been in control of history.
27-29	The real reason for the persecution of Christians is their refusal to sacrifice to the Emperor. However, the Romans are inconsistent in their religious observances. They pay more honor to mortal Caesar than to the deities. Further, no real benefit is derived from such sacrifices.
30-35	Although Christians may not pray to the Emperor as a deity, they do pray for him. Augustus himself refused to be treated as a deity. Despite this, Christians are persecuted for their refusal to worship the Emperor.
36-45	Christians deserve better treatment than they receive for they do no one harm and seek to do good to all. Yet they are blamed for the ills of society. Tertullian enumerates the many Christian virtues.
46-50	Christianity, whose teachings are prohibited, is compared to philosophy, which is acceptable. Philosophy is characterized as given to idle speculation but is taken seriously while Christianity, which is reasonable, is an object of derision. However, God will judge rightly in the end. Finally, Christians conquer even in their suffering.

Tertullian demonstrates a knowledge of Roman history and tradition throughout the *Apology*. Further, he makes reference to authors such as Diodorus and Thallus (ch. 10), and Seneca and Diogenes (ch. 50), and is aware of opinions of Zeno (ch. 20) and the Cybele (chs. 15 and 25). He is acquainted not only with myths and traditions of Rome but also of Persia (ch. 9), Athens, and Carthage (ch. 50).

Beginning in chapter 16, Tertullian confronts calumnies against the Church. The author admits that these misunderstandings pertain to both Christianity and Judaism. Therefore, Tertullian must clear Judaism of these charges in order to redeem Christianity.

In chapter 19 we encounter a familiar theme: Not only are the Jews an ancient people but their sacred literature antedates the literature of the Greeks. Tertullian reminds his Roman readers that a Greek translation of the Hebrew Bible was commissioned by Ptolemy Philadelphus (ch. 18). He lays claim to the authority of these writings and the prophetic tradition beginning with Moses on the basis of their great antiquity (ch. 19). Moses, according to Tertullian, antedates Homer by 500 years. The age of the Jewish religion is attested by the writings of the most ancient civilizations: Egypt, the Chaldeans, and Phoenicia.

As witnesses to the Jews, chapter 19 mentions Manetho the Egyptian, Berosus the Chaldean, King Hiram of Tyre, Ptolemy of Mendes, Demetrius Phalereus, King Juba, Apion, and Thallus. Tertullian recognizes that all these writers did not extoll the Jews but they all did attest to their antiquity and thus, indirectly, to the authority of their writings. He introduces "the Jew Josephus, the native vindicator of the ancient history of the Jews, who either provides verification or refutes them [i.e., the above-mentioned writers]."[5] In this discussion of the antiquity of the Jews, chapter 19 evinces acquaintance with *Against Apion.* However, Tertullian does not slavishly reproduce Josephan material but borrows freely from it and other sources to construct his own argument. Moses can be traced back to the time of the Argive king Inachus and he antedated Danaus, an ancient king of Argos, by almost 400 years. Josephus (*C.A.* 1.103 and 2.16) notes that Moses left Egypt 393 years before Danaus went to Argos. Tertullian mentions that Moses antedated the death of Priam by 1000 years while Josephus states only that Moses preceded the Trojan War by almost a millennium (*C.A.* 1.104). As in *C.A.,* Tertullian notes that the histories of Egypt, the Chaldeans, and the Phoenicians testify to the antiquity of the Jews (cf. *C.A.* 2.1). His list of authorities does not follow the Josephan order. Manetho is to be found in *C.A.* 1.73-105, 270-287, 293-303 and 2.1. The Chaldean Berosus is treated in 1.129-153. The Phoenician King Hiram and his relationship with Israel is considered in 1.106-126 and 2.18. Josephus mentions letters from Hiram to Solomon which supposedly yet existed (*C.A.* 1.111). Demetrius Phalereus is mentioned in 1.218 and in 2.46. Apion is considered at length in 2.8-144 and 295 while Thales (θάλητα) is mentioned in 1.14. Interestingly, Tertullian's reference to Thallus in the list of authors who wrote about the Jews appears to be an error on the part of the former who

---

[5]PL 1:445: "qui istos aut probat aut revincit, Judaeus Josephus antiquitatum Judaicarum vernaculus vindex."

mistook Thales for Thallus while reading *Against Apion* 1.14.[6] Further, Tertullian mentions both Ptolemy of Mendes and King Juba who are not mentioned in *Against Apion*. Ptolemy of Mendes is known through a citation in Tatian (*Ad Graec.* 38) in which Ptolemy dates Moses as a contemporary of Inachus, king of Argos (FGrH 4:485). This would appear to be the origin of the reference to Inachus in chapter 19 and would explain his presence in Tertullian's list of historians. The presence of the Libyan King Juba in Tertullian's list is more difficult to explain. Although Juba is not found in *C.A.*, he is to be discovered in *B.J.* 2.115 and *A.J.* 17.349 where he is the husband of Glaphyra, the daughter-in-law of Herod. Juba was a prolific author whose works are known primarily through fragments in Tacitus, Strabo, and especially Pliny (FGrH 3:465-484). Among the nine titles known are works on the history and culture of the Middle East. Although we do not know what he might have written of the Jews, it is plausible that he did write about them. That he was evidently esteemed by Greek and Roman writers may explain his presence in Tertullian's list of historians.

Summary

Tertullian demonstrates familiarity with *Against Apion* in his *Apology*. Although he does not cite any Josephan text, the apologist presents Josephus as the arch-defender of his people for it is he whom Tertullian declares to be the "vindicator" of the Jewish people. Tertullian's list of ancient writers appears to be drawn for the most part from *C.A.*, although Ptolemy of Mendes and Juba are not mentioned in *Against Apion* and Tertullian mistakes Thales for Thallus. Tertullian's knowledge of Josephan material stands in contrast with Minucius Felix whose work is somehow linked with Tertullian and whose familiarity with Josephus cannot be ascertained.

---

[6]It is not known whether Thallus indeed wrote anything negative about the Jews. Thallus wrote a three-volume history which covered the time from the fall of Troy to Ol. 167 (112-109 B.C.E.). See FGrH 2.B:1156-1158.

Chapter Nine

Hippolytus

Although Hippolytus stands as a very significant figure in the Roman Church, details about him remain elusive. Eusebius provides us with a bibliography (*H.E.* 6.22) which mentions Hippolytus' *Hexaëmeron, Against Marcion, On the Pascha, Against All Heresies,* and works on the Song of Solomon and Ezekiel. Although Hippolytus was purported to be a bishop, Eusebius does not know his see (*H.E.* 6.20). One other reference in Eusebius (*H.E.* 6.46) mentions that a certain Hippolytus bore a letter from Dionysius to the Roman Church. Whether this is our Hippolytus remains a mystery.

Hippolytus, born in the East, was resident in Rome and was active during the first decades of the third century C.E. He died c. 235. Hippolytus was possibly a student of Irenaeus, and his statue, discovered in Rome in 1551, describes him as bishop of Portus. He rigorously opposed leniency toward sinners and, on account of his position, was elected anti-Pope in opposition to Callistus (217-222 C.E.). He remained in schism under Urban and Pontianus. Eventually he was reconciled to the Roman Church and died in exile with Pontianus on Sardinia.[1]

Of particular interest to us is his ten volume work *Against All Heresies* (Κατὰ πασῶν αἱρέσεων ἔλεγχος or *Refutatio omnium haeresium*)[2]

---

[1] For a complete record of all references to Hippolytus in the literature and a description of the archaeological material see A. Harnack, *Geschichte der altchristlichen Litteratur bis Eusebius* (Leipzig, 1893), 2:605-619.

[2] This is the title most used by editions of the work. The edition used here is that of Paul Wendland (*Hippolytus Werke. Dritter Band. Refutatio omnium haeresium,* GCS 26 [Leipzig, 1916]). Although a general consensus exists that Hippolytus of Rome authored this work, P. Nautin (*Hippolyte et Josipe. Contribution a l'histoire de la littérature chrétienne du troisième siècle* [Paris, 1947]; also see *RSR* 42 [1954], 226-257) divided those books attributed to Hippolytus into works by an unknown Josipe who is to have written the *Philosophoumena, De Universo,* and the *Chronicle* during the first decades of the third century C.E. Other works are products of an unknown Christian from the East named Hippolytus. For Nautin, there existed certain doctrinal issues, especially regarding the Holy Spirit, and particulars of style which called into question the attribution of the *Philosophoumena* to Hippolytus. Nautin noted similiarities regarding Jewish chronology between book 10 and an anonymous ms entitled Συναγωγὴ χρόνων.

discovered at Mt. Athos in 1842. The Greek manuscript of *Against All Heresies* discovered was recognized as the continuation of a fragment erroneously attributed to Origen.[3]

The *Philosophoumena* (Φιλοσοφούμενα), as the work is also commonly known, consists of two parts (books 1-4 and books 5-9). The first part attempts to show that heretics drew their doctrines not from Christian teaching but from pagan thought. The title *Philosophoumena* is derived from the content of this section which deals with pagan wisdom. In books 1 and 2, the author summarizes, without betraying profound understanding, concepts from many different philosophers and authors.[4] Books 2 and 3 are not extant but book 4 deals with astrology and magic. The second part of the work, books 5-9, contains a description of the various heresies which comprise thirty-three Gnostic systems. Book 10 is a summary of the opinions of the philosophers and the heretics treated in the two preceding sections.

Josephus and Hippolytus

In book 9 of the *Philosophoumena* the author deals with Noetism, based on certain tenets of Heraclitus, which denied any difference between the material and the immaterial. Noetus' heresy rejected the distinction between the first two persons of the Trinity claiming that the Father and Son were really one. Hippolytus recites the personal histories of the wretched Callistus and Zephyrinus. Callistus' conduct and Zephyrinus' intellectual ability affirm the error of their heretical doctrine. Hippolytus then passes to the example of Elchasai whose false teaching is derived from Pythagoras. Elchasai, according to Hippolytus, requires his followers to submit to circumcision and observe the Law. Further, Elchasai asserts that Christ was but a mortal who, transferring

---

The similarities led Nautin to assume common authorship and, as there was no question that the latter ms was by Hippolytus, Nautin rejected Hippolytan authorship of the *Philosophoumena*. Further, certain similarities to a work (Περὶ τῆς τοῦ παντὸς οὐσίας) mentioned by Photius and attributed to a certain Josephus (not Flavius Josephus) led Nautin to this re-identification of the work. Nautin's book also recounts the history of the scholarship on the *Philosophoumena*. Objections to Nautin's novel thesis were raised by M. Richard (*MScR* 7 [1950], 237-268; *MScR* 8 [1951], 19-51; *MScR* 10 [1953], 13-52 and 145-180). For a more extensive bibliography on Nautin's thesis and objections to it, see B. Altaner, *Patrology*, 5th ed., trans. H. C. Graef (Freiburg, 1960), 185.
[3]Harnack, 2:625, *Geschichte der altchristlichen Litteratur bis Eurebius,* and Altaner, 184f.
[4]In I, Introduction 1-10 the author lists the relevant authorities: Thales, Pythagoras, Empedocles, Heraclitus, Anaximander, Anaximenes, Anaxagoras, Archelaus, Parmenides, Leucippus, Democritus, Xenophanes, Ecphantus, Hippo, Socrates, Plato, Aristotle, Chrysippus, Zeno, Epicurus, Phyrho, the Indian Brahmins, the Celtic Druids, and Hesiod. In the course of his narrative, the author mentions others as well.

his soul from body to body, would occasionally become incarnate. Astrology and magic are of great importance to this doctrine and knowledge thereof was to be jealously guarded.

Having dealt with various Greek philosophies and the heresies derived from them, Hippolytus concludes his work with a description of Judaism (book 9, chapters 18-31) out of a desire for comprehensiveness (chapter 17). As with the heresies, Hippolytus' view of Judaism is that of a fragmented group of sects related to Christianity but in conflict with the truth. The author depicts Judaism as having originally been one religion which later evolved into three sects: the Essenes, the Pharisees, and the Sadducees (chapter 18). Hippolytus gives more attention to the Essenes who are said to be devotional and loving in their relationships. Of greatest interest to Hippolytus are the doctrines of the three sects regarding the resurrection of the dead. Otherwise the author is generally interested in social customs rather than doctrinal issues.

An analysis of chapters 18-31 shows a close resemblance to *B.J.* 2.119-166.[5] Hippolytus appears to have closely followed Josephus' narrative with regard to content and order of material. Although Hippolytus includes material not found in the *B.J.*, the resemblance is remarkable. This led most scholars, beginning with Miller who was first to edit the text of the *Philosophoumena*, to presume dependence upon the Josephan narrative.[6] However, because of the differences between the *Philosophoumena* and the *B.J.*, Dunker suggested a common source. Cruice noted that the Essenes' doctrine of the resurrection in the *Philosophoumena* more closely resembles the concept of Christians (who pray for all and forgive their enemies while asserting the bodily resurrection) than that of Josephus' Essenes (who hate their enemies and the wicked while believing in the afterlife of the spirit).[7] Matthew Black also proposed an intermediary source which would account for the many differences between what we read in the *Philosophoumena* and the *B.J.*[8] Because of the considerable differences between the two, Black saw two options: Either both used a common source or Hippolytus utilized a version of Josephus quite different from that we presently possess. Black preferred the former option for several reasons: Since Josephus depicts the Essenes as sun-worshipers and as looking forward to

---

[5]*A.J.* 18.11-22 contains a more cursory treatment of the material from *B.J.* 2.119-166. Hippolytus' narrative demonstrates familiarity with material contained only in the longer account from the *Jewish War*.

[6]E. Miller, *Originis Philosophoumena* (Oxford, 1851), 297. For a general bibliography see Altaner, 184f. Nautin's *Hippolyte et Josipe* includes a history of early scholarship on the *Philosophoumena* (pp. 20-35).

[7]L. Dunker and F. Schneidewin, *S. Hippolyti . . . Refutationis Omnium Haeresium* (Göttingen, 1859), 10:472n. and P. Cruice, *Philosophoumena* (Paris, 1860), 460n.

[8]M. Black, "The Account of the Essenes in Hippolytus and Josephus", in *The Background of the New Testament and its Eschatology*, eds. W. D. Davies and D. Daube (Cambridge, 1956), 172-175.

the immortality of the spirit rather than to the resurrection of the dead, Black posited that we are looking at an account that was fashioned for a hellenistic audience. The account in the *Philosophoumena,* on the other hand, depicts the Essenes as more typically Jewish (i.e., less obviously influenced by Hellenism) in their devotion and beliefs. Further, the *Philosophoumena* provides a number of credible details not present in the *B.J.* These will be enumerated as we consider a comparison of the two works in detail. However, the additional information found in the *Philosophoumena* strikes Black as being credible and more likely inherent in a source used by both Josephus and Hippolytus than in an unknown version of the *B.J.* On behalf of Black's argument, it can be said that a third option, that Hippolytus used both Josephus and a second source from which he drew material and interpolated it into the Josephan material, would have been atypical for the *Philosophoumena.* Diels' analysis of Hippolytus' use of literature in the *Philosophoumena* indicates that he followed his sources closely.[9] Thus this third option would have been out of character for Hippolytus.

Morton Smith provided an detailed comparison of the relevant passages from the *Philosophoumena* and the *B. J.*[10] The differences examined by Smith fall in six areas: (1) The *Philosophoumena* notes that there are four different kinds of Essenes while Josephus informs us of the four grades in the sect akin to postulancy, the novitiate and profession in a Christian religious order. (2) To Josephus, the Essenes were martyred for their convictions confident that even the righteous are made more perfect by their death. This entire section on martyrdom (in the aorist) is absent in the *Philosophoumena.* (3) The *B.J.* makes it clear that the Essenes hold to the continued existence of the soul. Josephus likens the belief of the Essenes to that of the Greeks. The Essenes of the *Philosophoumena,* like the Pharisees, hold to a bodily resurrection of the dead. (4) Josephus' transition in *B.J.* 2.162 from the Essenes to the Pharisees returns to the subject of the Pharisees as if the material on the Essenes between 2.119 and 162 were not there. The description of the Essenes seems out of place. However, in the *Philosophoumena,* this is not the case. (5) Josephus is cursory in his treatment of the Sadducees while the *Philosophoumena* contains considerable information. (6) Finally, the Sadducees do not appear in the *B.J.* while they *are* considered in the *Philosophoumena.*

Like Black, Smith postulates a common source for both the Josephan and Hippolytan works. However, Smith is more specific with regard to the nature of that source. For Smith, the entire section in the *B.J.* which deals with the three Jewish sects is a digression. The context in which we read of the Essenes, Pharisees, and Sadducees is one which concerns the removal of Archelaus as ruler

---

[9]H. Diels, *Doxographii Graeci* (Berlin, 1879), 144ff.
[10]M. Smith, "The Description of the Essenes in Josephus and the Philosophoumena," *HUCA* 29 (1958), 273-313.

of Judea and the latter's transformation into a province under Coponius. During his procuratorship the revolt by Judas occurred. As Judas was the founder of a philosophical school, we arrive at a convenient place to discuss the three branches of Judaism.[11] Smith also sees this digression as being borrowed from an outside source. With the exception of the comment regarding how the Essenes resisted the Romans during war, the entire section is in the present tense though it is surrounded by material in the aorist. Thus Smith concludes that the material was borrowed from a source composed before 70 C.E.[12] After noting what appear to be Semiticisms in the Greek, Smith concludes that the source for both the *B.J.* and the *Philosophoumena* was a document of Gentile origins, possibly written in Aramaic, which described the Essenes, Pharisees, and Sadducees. Josephus tended to give primary importance to the Pharisees but used the material in the *B.J.* without serious editing. This would account for the description of the three groups being out of his unusual order.[13] Some of the references in the Josephan account may have been altered to suit his audience; however, a detail such as the Essenes' concern about excretion lest they outrage "the rays of the sun" (*B.J.* 2.148) may belong to the original. Hippolytus likewise borrowed from the same source and made alterations to suit his Christian audience.[14] Thus Smith explains the parallels and the differences between the *B.J.* and the *Philosophoumena*.[15]

As informative as is Morton Smith's analysis, Solomon Zeitlin's response is worthy of note.[16] Zeitlin denies that the material on the three sects of Judaism is a digression and insists that this is simply Josephus' style.[17] Zeitlin's point is that if it is not a digression, then it is likewise not an insertion copied from another source. Zeitlin is so concerned with upholding his own concept of the integrity of the Josephan text, that he cannot see or refuses to admit that such a digression is typical of Josephus. However, the absence of a digression no more proves that the material is genuinely Josephan than the existence of one guarantees that it was copied from another source. More

---

[11] Smith, 276-277.

[12] Smith, 279.

[13] Smith, 290-293.

[14] Smith, 289-290.

[15] G.W.E. Nickelsburg (*Resurrection, Immortality, and Eternal Life in Intertestamental Judaism*, Dissertation, Th.D., Harvard University Divinity School, Cambridge, Mass., 1967 [Cambridge, Mass., 1972], 350) is of the opinion that both Josephus and Hippolytus drew material from a common source for information regarding the immortality of the soul. C. Burchard ("Die Essener bei Hippolyt, Ref. IX 18,2-28,2 und Josephus, Bell. 2,119-161," *JSJ* 8 [1977], 1-41) admits a possible common source although Hippolytus was more likely directly dependent on Josephus.

[16] S. Zeitlin, "The Account of the Essenes in Josephus and the Philosophumenu," *JQR* 59 (1958-59), 292-299.

[17] Zeitlin, 293.

important is Zeitlin's point that certain typically Josephan vocabulary items in the *B.J.* are to be found in this section of *B.J.* 2. Of particular interest is that the term "the seventh day" is used while "the Sabbath" may be found in the *Philosophoumena*.[18] Further, the *Philosophoumena* mentions the Sicarii who were first introduced to Greek literature through Josephus.[19] Zeitlin rejects a common source to both the *B.J.* and the *Philosophoumena* in favor of an intermediate document of Christian origin which followed the *B.J.* closely. Important to Zeitlin is the fact that we possess no clear evidence which suggests the existence of another Palestinian source in Greek on the Essenes beyond Josephus. The existence of an intermediate document would explain the Christianization of the Essenes in the *Philosophoumena*. The material on the Sadducees and the Samaritans would have been a non-Josephan contribution of that intermediate Christian source. Zeitlin proposed that this unknown Christian work was by the second century Hegesippus whom we know from Eusebius (*H.E.* 4.8) to have composed a work on the Jewish sects, including Essenes, Pharisees, and Sadducees, around the time of the Bar-Kochba revolt.[20]

We are therefore faced with three options. The first is that the *B.J.* and the *Philosophoumena* shared a common source which they both followed closely with regard to subject matter, although edited to suit their audiences and general orientation. Thus Josephus hellenized the Essenes to cater to the ethnographic interests of his audience (which he did in any case although some of the hellenistic elements may have been original to the work) and Hippolytus made them appear more attractive to a Christian audience. To accept this hypothesis we must grant that this unknown document would have survived until the third century C.E. The more likely second option is that Hippolytus made use of a Christian work, such as that by Hegesippus, which followed the *B.J.* closely with regard to content but made additions and minimized the hellenistic elements in the Josephan narrative. If it is held that Josephus did indeed rely upon another work for his material on the three sects, the latter option is still not ruled out. A third and final option is that Hippolytus himself was responsible for altering the Josephan account. Since Hippolytus tended to follow his sources closely (as noted by Diels), it seems more likely that the Christianization of the Essenes came directly from his source rather than originating with himself.

In that we do not possess either a source which could have been utilized by both Josephus and Hippolytus or a work, such as that by Hegesippus, which could have revised Josephus' account of the Essenes in the *B.J.* and served Hippolytus as a source, we cannot solve this puzzle. Nevertheless, what we can say is that Hippolytus did not read Josephus' description of the Essenes in the

---

[18]Zeitlin, 294.
[19]Zeitlin, 298.
[20]Zeitlin, 295-296.

Jewish War and it seems likely that he used another source which relied on the *B.J.* If Hippolytus is transmitting Josephan material, it is only indirectly.

Chapter Ten

Origen

Origen is one of the best documented authors of the early Church. Eusebius, Pamphilus, Gregory Thaumaturgus, Photius, and Jerome provide information about his life and work.[1] Eusebius (*H.E.* 6) provides a complete biography of this Alexandrian who was born c. 185 C.E. and died c. 253. The ascetic Origen was influenced by the neo-Platonism of his native Alexandria, as is noticeable in his allegorical exegesis of Scripture. Origen was surrounded by controversy during his lifetime and much of his work was deemed unorthodox after his death. Jerome (*Adv. Ruf.* 2.22) claims that Origen wrote 2000 books of which many were collections of sermons. Only fragments of these remain in the original Greek and in Latin translation.

Although it is clear that Origen utilized Josephan material in his writings, the fragmentary nature of his extant works poses two problems. We cannot be certain how much of Josephus' writings may have been known by Origen in that we possess only a fraction of the latter's total literary output. Secondly, we cannot be certain whether Origen actually read Josephus or relied upon an intermediary source. Schreckenberg[2] identified several texts which suggest Josephan dependence but which are without attribution.

As an educator, Origen was noted for the inclusion of non-Christian literature in his course of study. In Christian circles the reading of philosophy was sanctioned for the purposes of refutation. However, Origen's students read hellenistic philosophy for its own merit. For Origen, truth was not confined to God's revelation in the Church but was to be found even in pagan literature.[3] Origen's works betray a knowledge of hellenistic literature from Plato to the Stoa.[4] With regard to Origen's interest in Judaism, his sources are less certain.

---

[1]A. Harnack, *Geschichte der altchristlichen Literatur bis Eusebius* (Leipzig, 1893), 1:332ff. and B. Altaner, *Patrology,* trans. H. Graef (Freiburg, 1960), 223ff.

[2]H. Screckenberg, *Die Flavius-Josephus-Tradition in Antike und Mittelalter* (Leiden, 1972) 73-76.

[3]René Cadiou, *La Jeunesse d'Origène: Histoire de l'Ecole d'Alexandrie au début du IIIe Siècle* (Paris, 1936), 70ff.

[4]Karl-Otto Weber (*Origenes der Neuplatoniker: Versuch einer Interpretation* [München, 1962]) provides an assessment of Origen's neoplatonism.

His fascination with Judaism is understandable given his exegetical interests. Few contemporaries concerned themselves with the Hebrew Bible but Origen's *Hexapla* indicates his interest in the Hebrew text and its relationship to the Greek tradition. Much of his information about Jewish tradition came from anonymous Jewish sources in Alexandria.[5] Origen was acquainted with Philo (*C. Cels.* 4.51; 6.21; *Comm. Mt.* 15.3) and Aristobulus (*C. Cels.* 4.51). Jerome (*de Vir.I.* 11) mentioned that Origen also knew Demetrius and Eupolemus.[6] Further, we shall see that it is unclear whether Origen gained knowledge of certain materials directly or through a third party.

In *Against Celsus*[7] (Κατὰ Κέλσῳ) 1.16, Origen mentions the two parts of Josephus' *Antiquities* (the second being *Against Apion*). This eight-book apology is a point-by-point refutation of Celsus' *A True Discourse* (Λόγος ἀληθής). Celsus accused Christianity of being a secret and illegal society which had invented the miraculous events described in the Gospels and whose religion was founded on barbarous Judaism. His attack on Christianity is made through the figure of a Jew. This is not to suggest that Celsus admired Judaism but that Christianity was viewed by him as a perversion of an already perverse race. Not only must Origen defend the integrity of Christian Scripture and correct Celsus' misinterpretation of Christian doctrine and practice, but he must fend off the attacks of Celsus against Judaism as the parent of Christianity. Origen attests to the antiquity of the Jewish people together with the Egyptians and Phoenicians and to Moses' place among the learned men of antiquity. Josephus' name is mentioned as an authority on Jewish antiquity. Likewise, *C. Cels.* 4.11 points to the same two books to illustrate that, owing to Moses' antiquity, the biblical account of the Flood, attributed to Moses, is more reliable than that of the Greek historians.

In *C. Cels.* 2.13, Origen notes that Josephus construes the destruction of Jerusalem as retribution for the murder of James, the brother of Jesus. Although Josephus does mention James' death at the hands of the high priest (*A.J.* 20.200), he does not in any way connect it to the destruction of Jerusalem by the Romans under Titus. Perhaps Origen's text of the *Antiquities* contains a Christian gloss on the pericope or possibly Origen is the source for the gloss.

Josephus' reference to James is also an issue in Origen's commentary on Matthew[8] (*Comm. Mt.* 10.17) with the same information found in the Latin

---

[5]N. R. M. de Lange, "Jewish Influence on Origen," in *Origeniana: premier colloque international des etudes origeniennes Monserrat 18-21 Septembre 1971*, ed. H. Crouzel, G. Lomiento and J. Rivs-Camps (Bari, 1975), 225ff.

[6]N. R. M. de Lange, *Origen and the Jews: Studies in Jewish Christian Relations in Third-Century Palestine* (Cambridge, 1976), 16.

[7]P. Koetschau, ed. *Origenes Werke. Erster Band. Die Schrift vom Martyrium. Buch I-IV gegen Celsus*, GCS 2 (Leipzig, 1899).

[8]E. Klostermann, ed., *Origenes Werke. Zehnter Band. Origenes Matthäuserklärung*, GCS 40 (Leipzig, 1935).

translation which contains material no longer extant in the Greek (*Comm. ser.* 25).[9] While discussing Jesus' family, Origen notes that Josephus wrote the history of the Jews in twenty books and attributes to Josephus the tradition that the death of James was the cause of Jerusalem's destruction.

Jewish resistance to the placing of effigies of the emperor in Jerusalem by Pilate (*B.J.* 2.169ff. and *A.J.* 18.55ff.) appears to have been known to Origen (*Comm. Mt.* 17.25). Origen, however, has the images not merely in the city but in the Temple area itself. We shall see this interesting variation again in the *Preparation for the Gospel* (8.2.122) of Eusebius, himself a student of Origen.

With reference to the murder of the innocent Zechariah son of Berachiah (Mt 23:35), who is unidentified in the Gospel, Origen claims that Josephus identified this Zechariah as the father of John the Baptist (Katenen fragment 457 II).[10] Josephus (*B.J.* 4.335-344) does mention the murder by the Zealots of "Zecharias, son of Baris" (Ζαχαρίαν υἱὸν Βάρεις in 335) relating that he was falsely accused of treasonous communication with the Romans during the siege of Jerusalem. Origen's identification appears based solely on the similarity of the two names.

In his commentary on the fourth Gospel (*Comm. Jn.* 6.9),[11] Origen refers to the revolts of Theudas and Judas the Galilean against the Romans. Origen may be thinking of Josephus' account of their uprisings (*A.J.* 20.97-102). However, if this is the case he errs in that Josephus makes it clear that Judas the Galilean revolted during the time of the census while Theudas' uprising occurred during the procuratorship of Fadus (c. 44 C.E.). Josephus does, however, mention that two sons of Judas were executed after Theudas' revolt. It is possible that Origen misread the Josephan narrative and confused the chronology or misread the reference regarding the execution of the two sons. It seems more likely, however, that Origen's information is derived not from Josephus but from Acts. The debate over whether the author of Acts made use of this same material from *A.J.* 20 or had another source is not our concern and yet, if both the author of Acts and Origen had access to the *A.J.*, then they made the same error. In both Origen's commentary and Gamaliel's speech in Acts 5, the speakers refer to the revolt of Theudas and "after him rose Judas the Galilean in the days of the census":

Acts 5:37: μετὰ τοῦτον ἀνέστη Ἰούδας ὁ Γαλιλαῖος ἐν ταῖς ἡμέραις τῆς ἀπογραφῆς

---

[9] E. Klostermann, ed., *Origenes Matthäuserklärung. II. Die lateinischen Übersetzung des commentariorum series*, GCS 38 (Leipzig, 1933).

[10] E. Klostermann, ed., *Origenes Werke. Zwölfter Band. Origenes Matthäuserklärung. III. Fragmente und Indices, 1. Hälfte*, GCS 41.1 (Leipzig, 1941).

[11] E. Preuschen, ed., *Origenes Werke. Vierter Band. Der Johanneskommentar*, GCS 10 (Leipzig, 1903).

Comm. Jn. 6.9: μετ ' ἐκεῖνον 'Ιούδας ὁ Γαλιλαῖος ἐν ταῖς τῆς ἀπογραφῆς ἡμέραις

Despite the brevity, there are noticeable verbal similarities. Origen merely dropped the verb as it was not necessary in his sentence and rearranged a phrase. It seems more likely that he was dependent on Acts 5 than upon Josephus. The question of whether this makes Origen indirectly dependent upon *A.J.* rests with the determination of the relationship between Acts and *A.J.*.

Jn. Comm. 13.39 (on John 4:35) deals with the Passover and the Feast of Unleavened Bread. Although the content of the reference to the two festivals parallels that of Lev 23:6, Origen notes that the Passover occurs during the month of Nisan. Lev does not do this but Josephus does (*A.J.* 3.248 and 249). However, we should not assume that Josephus was the sole source for Origen's knowledge of the Jewish calendar. Origen's Jewish sources, albeit unidentified, were certainly more extensive than Josephus alone.

In his commentary on Lamentations (*Comm. Lam.* 105 with reference to Lam 4:10),[12] Origen seeks to relate the privations and calamities following the Babylonian capture of Jerusalem to the state of affairs in the city accompanying the Roman siege. Lam 4:10 deals with the cannibalism of children at the hands of their mothers which Origen notes occurred during the Roman siege of Jerusalem. Josephus (*B.J.* 6.201-213) records such an event which occurred during the siege of the city. That Origen was indeed thinking of the Josephan account is rendered probable by his comments on Lam 4:14 (*Comm. Lam.* 109) in which he describes the noise and the voice heard one night by the priests serving before the altar in the inner court of the Temple and which closely parallel the episode appearing in the *Jewish War:*

> *B.J.* 6.299 (Niese): At night the priests entering into the inner court of the Temple, as was their custom for the liturgy, reported that they were first aware of a commotion and of a sound and afterwards the voice as of a host: "We are departing hence."

> *Comm. Lam.* 109: At night the priests entering into the Temple, as was their custom for the liturgy, first reported a commotion and afterwards the voice as of a host: "We are departing hence."[13]

---

[12]E. Klostermann, ed., *Origenes Werke. Dritter Band. Jeremiahomolien, Klageliederkommentar. Erklärung der Samuel und Königsbücher*, GCS 6 (Leipzig, 1901). We have already seen that Melito of Sardis drew a connection between Lamentations and the Roman siege of Jerusalem.

[13]*B.J.* 6.299: 'νύκτωρ οἱ ἱερεῖς παρελθόντες εἰς τὸ ἔνδον ἱερὸν, ὥσπερ αὐτοῖς ἔθος πρὸς τὰς λειτουργίας, πρῶτον μὲν κινήσεως ἔφασαν ἀντιλαβέσθαι καὶ κτύπου, μετὰ δὲ ταῦτα φωνῆς ἀθρόας 'μεταβαίνομεν ἐντεῦθεν.' *Comm. Lam.* 109: νύκτωρ οἱ ἱερεῖς παρελθόντες εἰς τὸ ἱερόν, ὥσπερ αὐτοῖς ἔθος ἦν πρὸς τὰς λειτουργίας, πρῶτον μὲν κινήσεως ἔφασαν ἀντιλαμβάνεσθαι, μετὰ δὲ ταῦτα φωνῆς ἀθρόας· μεταβαίνωμεν ἐντεῦθεν·

The close similarity between Josephus' and Origen's accounts would indicate that Origen either had *B.J.* before him or possessed another work which contained the Josephan account. More remotely, of course, is the possibility that both Josephus and Origen were dependent on a common source.

Regarding Lam 4:19 (*Comm. Lam.* 115), Origen deals with the identity of those fleeing Jerusalem and being waylaid in the wilderness. Origen notes cryptically that "Josephus recorded the story of those who fled into the hills."[14] Schreckenberg suggests that this is a reference to Josephus' account of inhabitants of besieged Jerusalem who abandoned the city to search for food and who were captured by the Romans and crucified (*B.J.* 5.446ff.).[15] Schreckenberg's suggestion is plausible but Origen's comments bear little relationship to the Josephan material.

In Origen's homily on Jeremiah (fragment nr. 14 on Jer 22:24-26),[16] the author mentions the report of "Josephus in the tenth book of the *Antiquities*" (Ἰώσηππος ἐν τῇ δεκάτῃ τῆς ἀρχαιολογίας) regarding Jehoiakim. Origen summarizes the salient features of *A.J.* 10.81-98 in which Eliakim is made king by the Egyptian king Necho who changes his name to Jehoikim. Jehoikim is eventually killed by the Babylonians who cast his body outside the gates of Jerusalem. As Origen does not clearly identify his source, it is impossible to determine if this material was derived directly from Josephus or another party.

In his commentary on the Song of Songs[17] (*Cant. Cantic.* II), Origen recounts the visit to Solomon of the Queen of Sheba, who ruled both Egypt and Ethiopia. Origen draws a connection between Sheba and the city of Saba in Ethiopia which was renamed by Cambyses after his sister Meroe. In *A.J.* 8.165ff. the queen is described as the ruler of both Egypt and Ethiopia, a claim not made by either Kings or Chronicles, and *A.J.* 2.249 relates that the Ethiopian capital Saba was renamed Meroe by Cambyses upon conquering Ethiopia. Baehrens' edition of the commentary is based on the incomplete Latin translation of Rufinus which makes the determination of direct or indirect literary dependence a dubious enterprise.

In his homily on Ps 73 (PG 12.1529), Origen treats the pride of the wicked and the violence perpetrated by them (v. 6). He maintains that, in his account of the capture of Jerusalem, Josephus narrated the punishment of the wicked. This theological perspective on Josephus' account is not far removed from Josephus' own viewpoint.

---

[14] Ἱστορεῖ γὰρ Ἰώσηππος ὡς οὐδὲ τὰ ὄρη τοὺς φεύγοντας διέσωσεν.

[15] Schreckenberg, 74.

[16] E. Klostermann, ed., *Origenes Werke. Dritter Band. Jeremiahomolien, Klageliederkommentar. Erklärung der Samuel und Königsbücher*, GCS 6 (Leipzig, 1901).

[17] W. A. Baehrens, ed., *Origenes Werke. Achter Band. Homolien zu Samuel I, zum Hohelied und zu den Propheten. Kommentar zum Hohelied in Rufinus und Hieronymus' Übersetzung*, GCS 33 (Leipzig, 1925).

In a homily on Genesis 17 (PG 12.258) extant only in a Latin translation, Origen makes reference to Gen 49:10. Origin points out that the scepter (which would not pass from Judah until laid at the feet of him who deserved it) belonged to Jesus, not the Herodians. Herod's illegal claim to rule can, according to Origen, be demonstrated from the writings of Josephus. Josephus deals with the Idumean origins and the intrigues of Antipater and his son Herod in *A.J.* 14.8ff.

Summary

With respect to Josephan literature, it is difficult to assess precisely when Origen might be using a source directly or through a third party. He expands on the Josephan tradition by asserting that the destruction of Jerusalem was in response to the death of James. He also has Pilate placing effigies of the emperor in the Temple rather than merely in the city. Where the Josephan tradition has been embellished, we might see the hand of an intermediate source. However, it is just as likely that Origen was responsible for the embellishment. In his commentary on John, Origen follows Acts rather than *A.J.* in his chronology of the revolts of Theudas and Judas the Galilean. Only once (*Comm. Lam.* 109) does Origen's text bear close verbal similarity to Josephan material (*B.J.* 6.299). Origen may have also gleaned further information from Josephan sources and employed it elsewhere. Origen does not provide us with enough information to say whether he drew his knowledge directly from Josephus or through another source. What can be said, however, is that Origen deemed the Josephan material to be significant. In asserting the antiquity and authority of Judaism, he was thereby doing the same for Christianity. We shall see this theme more fully developed by Eusebius, who was greatly influenced by Origen. Further, Origen saw in Josephus confirmation and explication of New Testament tradition. Whether Origen utilized Josephus directly or not does not alter his understanding of the significance of the material.

Chapter Eleven

Methodius

Methodius, bishop of Olympus, is reputed to have been martyred during the Diocletian persecution c. 311 C.E.[1] We know no more than this about him assuming that even this information is accurate. Methodius as a writer was also fated for obscurity. As early as the fourth century, according to Harnack, "Methodius' fate was to be literarily plundered."[2] Works composed by him were attributed to other writers. Nevertheless, as obscure as he remains to us, he did exercise some influence on Christian literature. Citations, although frequently unattributed, may be found in Eusebius, Epiphanius, Jerome, Socrates, John of Damascus and Photius.[3] What can be said for Methodius is that he was a noted opponent of Origen and that his literary efforts anticipated the official censure of Origenism to come.

On the Resurrection or the *Aglaophon* (τοῦ ἁγιου Μεθοδίου περὶ ἀναστάσεως or τοῦ ἁγ. Μ. ᾿Αγλαοφῶν) is extant in three fragmentary books. The work attempts to refute Origen's doctrine of the pre-existence of the soul and his refusal to identify the resurrected form with a physical body. In *On the Resurrection* 3.9 (found in Photius' *Bibliotheca* 234.300b.18-41), Methodius defends the notion that the resurrection of the dead is present in Ezekiel 37. Since Origen denied the physical resurrection, he viewed Ezekiel's pronouncements on the revivification of the dry bones as pertaining not to the the resurrection of the dead but to the return from the Babylonian exile. In order to demonstrate the fallacy of this allegorical exegesis, Methodius cites *B.J.* 6.435-437:

> And this was recorded by Josephus who says: Jerusalem was captured in the second year of Vespasian's reign and it had been captured five times earlier. It was destroyed for the second time. For Asochaeus, king of the

---

[1] Jerome, *Vir. Ill.* 83, and Socrates, *H.E.* 6.13. See V. Buchheit's *Studien zu Methodius von Olympos* (TU 69 [Berlin, 1958]).

[2] A. Harnack, *Geschichte der altchristlichen Litteratur bis Eusebius* (Leipzig, 1893), 1:470: ". . . ist Methodius dem Schicksal verfallen, literarisch ausgeplündert zu werden."

[3] G. N. Bonwetsch, *Methodius,* GCS 27 (Leipzig, 1917), IX-XVII. It is Bonwetsch's edition of *On the Resurrection* which will be employed here.

Egyptians, and thereafter Antiochus, next Pompey, and after these Sossios, with Herod, took the city and burnt it. But before these the king of the Babylonians captured and destroyed it. *On the Resurrection* 3.9.15-21[4]

Methodius finds Origen's logic unacceptable since the returnees to Jerusalem at the time of Cyrus were still a subject people and took forty-six years to rebuild what Solomon had accomplished in seven. In short, God's promise to Israel was not yet fulfilled. Further, as the destruction of Jerusalem in the sixth century B.C.E. was but the first of two, Methodius deems it unacceptable to interpret the return to Jerusalem as anything resembling the resurrection of the dead which he sees as a once-and-for-all event. Origen's exegesis of the passage takes too many liberties with the Church's understanding of the resurrection.

The text in Niese's edition differs in that Jerusalem was captured "in the second year of Vespasian's reign on the eighth of the month Gorpiaeus" and when Herod and Sossios captured Jerusalem they did not burn (ἐνέπρησαν) the city but "preserved" (ἐτήρησαν) it.[5] This latter variant reading supports the imperfect Codex Laurentianus (eleventh century). In that the reading present in our text of Methodius contradicts the sense of the passage and given the similarity of both letters and sound between the two words, it seems reasonable to assume that this was a scribal error rather than an intentional alteration.

The significance of the *Jewish War* in this fragment of *On the Resurrection* says more for its importance to Origen than to Methodius. We have seen the relevance of the account of the siege of Jerusalem in the *Jewish War* to Origen in his commentary on Lamentations as well as his general use of Josephan material in his own works. Methodius could be refuting Origen's ideas using Origen's sources. Indeed, it is plausible that Methodius is responding to Origen's use of *B.J.* 6 in a lost exegetical work on Ezekiel 37. In any event, Methodius' citation from the *Jewish War* is little more than an appendix to Origen's use of the Jewish historian.

---

[4]καὶ τοῦτο Ἰώσηππος ἱστορεῖ λέγων »ἔτει δευτέρῳ τῆς Οὐεσπασιανοῦ ἡγεμονίας, ἁλοῦσα δὲ καὶ πρότερον πεντάκις, τοῦτο δεύτερον ἠρημώθη. Ἀσωχαῖος μὲν γὰρ ὁ τῶν Αἰγυπτίων βασιλεύς, καὶ μετ' αὐτὸν Ἀντίοχος, ἔπειτα Πομπήϊος, καὶ ἐπὶ τούτοις σὺν Ἡρώδῃ Σόσσιος ἐλόντες ἐνέπρησαν τὴν πόλιν· πρὸ δὲ τούτων ὁ τῶν Βαβυλωνίων βασιλεὺς κρατήσας ἠρήμωσεν αὐτήν.«

[5]*B.J.* 6.435: Ἑάλω μὲν ὄντως Ἱεροσόλυμα ἔτει δευτέρῳ τῆς Οὐεσπασιανοῦ ἡγεμονίας Γορπιαίου μηνὸς ὀγδόῃ . . . . 6.436: . . . καὶ ἐπὶ τούτοις σὺν Ἡρώδῃ Σόσσιος ἐλόντες ἐτήρησαν τὴν πόλιν.

Chapter Twelve

Lactantius

We now turn to a rather dubious use of the *Antiquities* by Lactantius in his *Divine Institutes*. Jerome informs us that Lactantius was a pupil of the African rhetorician Arnobius (*Vir. Ill.* 80). Lactantius was made a teacher of Latin rhetoric in Nicomedia by Emperor Diocletian. Having become a Christian, Lactantius was compelled to resign as a result of Diocletian's persecution of the Church. Lactantius went to the imperial court at Treves c. 317 C.E. when Constantine made Lactantius tutor of his son Crispus. We know nothing of his later life.

The *Divine Institutes (Divinae institutiones),* like the *Octavius* of Minucius Felix and the *Apology* of Tertullian, seek to illustrate the vanity of Greek philosophy and the truth of Christianity. Each book of the *Institutes* stands as an independent essay with its own title.

Book

1   "On the False Worship of Gods": Lactantius demonstrates the folly of worshipping the Greek deities. Lactantius points out the immorality and pettiness of the gods and the absurd attempt by the Stoics to reinterpret the myths.

2   "On the Origin of Error": Lactantius considers how humankind is ignorant of the true God whom they neglect in their prosperity. The author clearly distinguishes between God and the created order. Astrology and soothsaying are demonic in origin and God cannot be worshipped in the form of idols for He is greater than any object fashioned by mortal hand.

3   "On the False Wisdom of Philosophers": Greek philosophy failed to attain the truth expressed simply in Scripture.

4   "Of True Wisdom and Religion": Wisdom is inseparable from true religion. The wisdom of God manifested in the prophets and in the incarnate Word is presented.

5   "Of Justice": Lactantius explains how Christians and Christianity were unjustly condemned.

6   "Of True Worship": Lactantius compares the worship of the true
         God and the worship of false deities.

7   "Of a Happy Life": A happy life is attainable only through
         worship of the true God and not by worshipping false gods.
         Judgment awaits the pagan while resurrection and renewal of the
         world is promised to the Christian.

        E. R. Curtius noted that Lactantius made use of Josephus' interpretation
of Gen 6:2 in which Josephus understands the "sons of God" as angels and
compares their progeny with the giants of hellenistic myths (*A.J.* 1.73).[1]
Lactantius does indeed go beyond the biblical account in describing how God had
sent angels to earth to assist humankind (*Divine Institutes* 2.15). The angels
were dispatched with a prohibition against cohabitation with women which they
promptly disregarded having been enticed by the devil. Like Josephus,
Lactantius' exegesis depicts the offspring of the angels as evil, but there are
several factors which cause us to question Curtius' assumption that Lactantius
read the *Antiquities:* there is no verbal similiarity between the *Institutes* and the
Antiquities, and the accounts have more dissimilar characteristics than similar
ones. The activity of the devil who enticed the angels to cohabit with women is
entirely absent in the Josephan account. Further, Lactantius is concerned that
the angels could apparently flaunt God's authority. Thus God foresaw the
transgressions of the angels and prohibited what He knew they would do so that
they could not be forgiven afterward. Finally, in the *Institutes* the children of
the fallen angels are demons and are nowhere compared with giants as in
Antiquities.
        Further, even if Lactantius relied on an external source for his exegesis of
Gen 6:2, it need not have been *Antiquities.* Philo also understands the progeny
of the fallen angels to be giants (*Quaest. in Gen.* 1.92). Further, Schreckenberg
notes that Justin has this interpretation of Gen 6:2 (2 *Apol.* 5)[2] What we may
be seeing is evidence of an interpretation of Gen 6:2 common in late antiquity.
Given this and the dissimilarity of the accounts in the *Divine Institutes* and the
Antiquities, we must declare Curtius' conjecture that Lactatius read *Antiquities* as
improbable.

---

[1]E. R. Curtius, *Europäische Literatur und lateinisches Mittelalter,* 7th ed. (Bern,
1969), 226.
[2]H. Schreckenberg, *Rezeptionsgeschichte und textkritische Untersuchungen zu
Flavius Josephus* (Leiden, 1977), 26.

Chapter Thirteen

Eusebius Pamphili

Eusebius Pamphili marks both the end and the beginning of an era. This writer reflects the transition between a Church seeking legitimacy in itself and beyond its confines to one seeking to define itself in a position unimaginable only a few years earlier except in its eschatological dreams. However, the transition from persecuted to favored cult, if not yet the state religion, was not one without concern. If the Church had its detractors before Constantine's elevation of Christianity, it had them after as well. The Church was still too novel for hellenists who traced their roots back to Greek philosophers and prided themselves on their heritage of Greek myth and lore. Further, if by Constantine's favor the Church were freed from active persecution by the state, it now had to define its peculiar relationship to the state and respond to imperial intrusion into its affairs. Eusebius' greatness partly lies in his contribution to this transition period in the life of the Church.

We actually know little of the early life of this bishop of Caesaria (c. 265-340 C.E.) who was excommunicated at the synod of Antioch (325 C.E.) owing to his rejection of the proposed anti-Arian creed but who offered a compromise creed at Nicaea in the same year and made an uneasy truce with the Athanasians. A product of the Alexandrian school, he was a proponent of Origen's allegorical hermeneutic. Owing to his adherence to Origen's doctrine of subordination, Eusebius has been neither canonized nor made a Doctor of the Church despite his considerable contribution to Christian historical writing. Nevertheless, as a synthesist of historical tradition, he remains unsurpassed among Christian writers of late antiquity.[1]

A Note on Eusebius' Citations from Josephus

Eusebius cited a considerable amount of Josephan material and was generally faithful to his source, paraphrasing only seldom. The Josephan texts he utilized were eclectic and refuse to fit neatly into one of the families of manuscripts

---

[1] For a complete biographical statement, see the admirable article by Bishop Lightfoot in *A Dictionary of Christian Biography, Literature, Sects and Doctrine*, eds. W. Smith and H. Wace (London, 1880), 2:308-348. Also see A. Harnack, *Geschichte der altchristlichen Litteratur bis Eusebius* (Leipzig, 1893), 1:551-586.

identified by Niese.[2] One could suggest that Eusebius read Josephus partially through secondary sources as has been proposed by Gelzer who thought Julius Africanus provided Eusebius with Josephan material.[3] For our purposes it is not of critical importance if Eusebius cited Josephus directly from the primary texts or if he intentionally cited Josephus as transmitted by another source. If Eusebius preferred to cite Josephus through a secondary source rather than look up the citation, he was nevertheless cognizant of the origin of the material. Unresolved textual problems cannot blind us to the significance of Josephan literature for Eusebius' writings.

Eusebius' Works

With exception of two fragmentary works, *Prophetic Excerpts on Christ*[4] (Περὶ τοῦ Χριστοῦ προφητικαὶ ἐκλογαί) and the *Selection from Histories*[5] ('Εκλογὴ ἱστοριῶν), the latter being drawn from the *Chronicle,* the Josephan references appear in the large, and for the most part extant, works of Eusebius.

The *Ecclesiastical History*[6] ('Εκκλησιαστικὴ ἱστορία) presents Eusebius' grand design to explain the development of the Church from its origins as prophesied by the prophets to its ultimate triumph during the reign of Emperor Constantine despite many perils due to a hostile culture from without and heresies from within. It would be an error to see Eusebius' effort as a radical new interpretation of ecclesiastical history; rather, it is as an expression of self-awareness. The significance of Eusebius' history of the Church lies in its integration of existing intellectual currents in order to explain what appeared to the Church as the vindication of its proclamation to be the earthly expression of the Kingdom of God. The realization of the new problems facing the manifestation of the Kingdom in its alliance with the State, such as we find in Augustine's theology, was yet to be discovered. This history by Eusebius is the story of heroism and fulfillment.

---

[2] For an text-critical analysis of Josephan excerpts in Eusebius, see Eduard Schwartz, ed., *Eusebius Werke. Zweiter Band. Die Kirchengeschichte.* GCS 9.3 (Leipzig, 1909), cliii-clxxxvii. Also see Heinz Schreckenberg, *Die Flavius-Josephus-Tradition in Antike und Mitteralter* (Leiden, 1972), 85.

[3] Heinrich Gelzer, *Sextus Julius Africanus und die byzantische Chronographie* (Leipzig, 1885), 1:247-255; 2:31-37, 46-57, 63f.

[4] T. Gaisford, ed., *Ecologae Propheticae* in PG 22:1017-1262.

[5] In J. A. Cramer, ed., *Anecdota graeca e codd. manuscriptis bibliothecae regiae Parisiensis* (Oxford, 1839), 2:165-230.

[6] E. Schwartz and T. Mommsen, eds., *Eusebius Werke. Zweiter Band. Die Kirchengeschichte. Die Lateinische Übersetzung des Rufinus.* GCS 9.1-9.3 (Leipzig, 1903-1909). Schwartz edited the Greek and Mommsen the Latin translation by Rufinus.

Book

1   Jesus' birth is foretold by the prophets and his message is treated as non-revolutionary. Herod, Pilate and the high priests are described, as are the disciples.

2   The time from the Ascension to the beginning of the Jewish War is considered. Roman history is summarized and the ministries of Peter and Mark are discussed.

3   The Jewish War is considered at length, particularly the siege of Jerusalem. The Gospels and the deaths of the Apostles are treated, as is the development of the Church in Jerusalem and Rome.

4   The reign of Trajan is considered as are the heresies which afflicted the Church during that period. The martyrdom of Christians such as Polycarp and Justin is narrated. The development of the Antiochene Church and opinions of Melito are considered.

5   Christians are martyred in Gaul. The careers of Irenaeus and Clement of Alexandria are recounted and Montanism and the Marcionite heretics are discussed.

6   The continued persecution of the Church is described. The contributions of Clement of Alexandria, Origen, Ambrose and Julius Africanus to the Church are considered.

7   Cyprian and the persecution of the Church by Valerian are considered. The Manichean heresy is described as are the stories of Dionysius and the Egyptian Church.

8   The Church continues to undergo persecution and its sanctuaries are burned. A false peace comes to Christianity due to an imperial edict.

9   Relief to the persecuted Church comes through the victory of Constantine and Licinius.

10   Licinius proves to be wicked but Constantine is worthy of a panegyric by Eusebius.

The *Chronicle*[7] (Χρονικοὶ κανόνες ἐπιτομὴ παντοδαπᾶς ἱστορίας) comprises two parts. The first part consists of short histories of the various nations: the Chaldeans, the Hebrews, the Egyptians, the Greeks (including the Macedonians) and the Romans. Eusebius includes king lists for each nation. The second part of the *Chronicle* is a chronological tabulation of the major

---

[7] J. Karst, ed. and trans., *Eusebius Werke. Fünfter Band. Die Chronik aus dem Armenischen übersetzt mit textkritischen Commentar*, GCS 20 (Leipzig, 1911) and R. Helm, ed., *Eusebius Werke. Siebenter Band. Die Chronik des Hieronymus. Hieronymi Chronicon*, GCS 47 (Berlin, 1956).

events in history beginning with the birth of Abraham. The first part of the *Chronicle* is extant only in a sixth-century Armenian translation which includes the entire work while the second part, also in the Armenian translation, may also be found in a rather free Latin translation by Jerome who continued Eusebius' list to the year 378 C.E.

The *Onomasticon*[8] (Περὶ τῶν τοπικῶν ὀνομάτων τῶν ἐν τῇ θείᾳ γραφῇ) lists all place names found in the LXX and the Gospels. Eusebius, treating each letter of the Greek alphabet independently, lists the names grouped by biblical book in the order in which they occur, with a brief description of their location. Nu and Deut are treated as a single group. Under the heading of "Kings" fall 1-2 Sam, 1-2 Kgs, 1-2 Chr and the prophetic books. All four Gospels are also in one group. No other books of the New Testament are treated.

The *Preparation for the Gospel*[9] (Εὐαγγελικὴ προπαρασκευή) is less a work composed by Eusebius than an anthology of philosophical opinion compiled by him. The bishop lets recognized writers make his case for him while he directs the reader along a chosen line of thought. The fifteen books of the *P.E.* are divided into five groups of three books. The prefaces to books 1, 4, 7, 10 and 13 indicate the divisions and the introduction of book 15 summarizes the entire argument:

Books

1-3	The original fables regarding the deities are ridiculed by later Greek philosophers and poets.
4-6	The opinions of philosophers on fate and free will are considered and their fallacies are exposed.
7-9	The Hebrews based their opinions on the excellence of their sacred writings and accuracy of their recorded history.
10-12	The Greeks borrowed from Hebrew theology. Plato is treated as dependent upon Moses.
13-15	Moses is compared with Plato and opinions of various Greek philosophers are held up to criticism.

Eusebius continued the *Preparation for the Gospel* in his *Demonstration of the Gospel*[10] (Εὐαγγελικὴ ἀπόδειξις). As the *P.E.* argued that Judaism was

[8] E. Klostermann, ed., *Eusebius Werke. III. Band 1. Hälfte. Das Onomastikon der Biblischen Ortsnamen*, GCS 11.1 (Leipzig, 1904).
[9] K. Mras, ed., *Eusebius Werke. Achter Band. Die Praeparatio Evangelica*, GCS 8.1-8.2 (Berlin, 1954-1956).
[10] I. A. Heikel, ed., *Eusebius Werke. Sechster Band. Die Demonstratio Evangelica*, GCS 23 (Leipzig, 1913).

not to be despised but was philosophically and ethically superior to Hellenism, the *Demonstration* endeavored to show that Christianity was the heir to Judaism. The two works must be seen as parts of a single design. The bishop's argument is that Christianity is in all ways superior to paganism. However, the relative newness of the religion speaks against its claims in a culture where antiquity is a corollary to authority. Eusebius, therefore, must show that Christianity's mother faith, Judaism, enjoys superiority over its hellenistic counterparts but that it was only preparatory to Christianity. The Jewish Scriptures themselves stand witness to this as they predicted the Christ. Thus the pagans cannot make the claim that Christianity is too novel a religion to be taken seriously. Concomitantly, the virtues and especially the antiquity of Judaism become possessions of the Church. The *Demonstration of the Gospel* originally consisted of 20 books although only books 1-10 and a small fragment of 15 are extant.

Book

1   Eusebius introduces the work. The Gentiles were not included under the Mosaic constitution whereas Christ, who brought about the New Testament, is the author of salvation for all.

2   Jewish Scripture promised that mercy would be extended to the Gentiles.

3   Moses and the other Hebrew prophets had foreknowledge of Christ.

4   Scripture makes allusions to the divinity of Christ.

5   The salvation brought about by Christ was prophesied by Scripture.

6   Inferences in Scripture regarding Christ's sojourn among humankind are examined.

7   Eusebius presents prophecies regarding the Incarnation.

8   Judean history preceding the birth of Jesus is examined.

9   Prophecies regarding historical circumstances which occurred at the time of Jesus' birth are examined.

10   The opposition to Christ and his Passion were foreseen in Scripture.

On the Theophany[11] ($\Pi\epsilon\rho\grave{\iota}$ $\tau\hat{\eta}\varsigma$ $\theta\epsilon o\phi\alpha\nu\epsilon\acute{\iota}\alpha\varsigma$), extant only in a few Greek fragments but completely in a Syriac translation, is a rhetorical piece dealing

---

[11] H. Gressman, ed. and trans., *Eusebius Werke. III. Band 2. Hälfte. Die Theophanie. Die Griechischen Brüchstücke und Übersetzung der Syrischen Überlieferungen*, GCS 11.2 (Leipzig, 1904).

with the Incarnation and draws on both the *Preparation for the Gospel* and the *Demonstration of the Gospel.*

Book

1   Eusebius introduces the concept of the Logos and the incarnation of the Logos. The human task is to recognize mortal frailty in the face of the power of the divine Logos.

2   It was necessary for God to act on our behalf. The wisdom of the Greeks, along with the Egyptians and Phoenicians, has been to deify demons and commit idolatry which provide no aid to humankind.

3   Eusebius considers how the Savior has defeated the demonic forces and varied deities which had enslaved humanity. Christ has established his universal kingdom. All these things were foreseen by the Hebrew prophets. The Savior's work is advanced by his disciples throughout the world.

4   Eusebius recounts prophecies made by Jesus recorded in the Gospels. The triumph of the Church is promised but also the division of families, the martyrdom of the disciples and the rejection of the Jews along with the destruction of Jerusalem and the Temple. The destruction of the Temple is evidence that God's Law is now fulfilled solely in the Church. Eusebius cites Josephus' account of the privations of Jerusalem in the *B.J.* Jesus also predicts that deceivers would one day be included in the Church but would be gleaned out on the last day when all would be fulfilled.

5   Eusebius addresses those who take Christ to be a magician and a deceiver and whoever refuses to believe the disciples' accounts of the Savior's miraculous deeds. The *Testimonium Flavianum* is cited.

Josephus as Author and Authority

In his *Ecclesiastical History,* Eusebius informs his readers of Josephus' time and origins (*H.E.* 3.9.1-3 [222, 1-13]). He cites from the *Jewish War:* "Josephus, son of Matthias, a priest from Jerusalem, fighting against the Romans from the first of the war, and afterwards compelled to be present" (*B.J.* 1.3 in *H.E.* 3.9.1 [222, 1]). To Eusebius, Josephus was the most famous Jew of his age and his authority rested in the high esteem with with he was held by the Romans. Eusebius notes that he wrote a twenty-volume history of the Jews as well as a seven-volume account of the Jewish war. The latter appeared in his native tongue as well as in Greek. Eusebius also notes awareness of Josephus'

Eusebius Pamphili 75

appendix to the *Antiquities*, *Against Apion*, which he refers to as Περὶ τῆς Ἰουδαίων ἀχαιότητος (*On the Antiquity of the Jews*).

Eusebius also credits Josephus with the composition of 4 Maccabees and mentions Josephus' stated intent (*A.J.* 20.268) to write a four-volume work on the ancestral Jewish concept of God and the Law (*H.E.* 3.10.6-7 [224,16-24]). Eusebius fails to recognize that this apparently unrealized work is quite possibly *Against Apion* despite Josephus' title for the work. In the *Chronicle* of Jerome, Eusebius draws from *A.J.* 20.267 that Josephus was writing his *Antiquities* during the reign of Emperor Domitian (*Chron.* [Jerome]191.22-24).

Finally, Josephus is to be treated as a historical authority not merely because he lived through the events he related in his work on the Jewish war or because he was lauded by his Roman masters but because, as Eusebius discovers in the *Life*, his historical works were confirmed by King Agrippa and the Emperor Titus as to their accuracy (*V* 361-364; *H.E.* 3.10.9-11 [226, 7-18]).

Background to the New Testament

Not surprisingly, Eusebius' interest in documenting the history of the period immediately prior to and contemporary with the persons and events of the New Testament is most often visible in his *Ecclesiastical History*. For this purpose, Josephus serves as a major source of information. However, the *Demonstration of the Gospel* (which shows the preparatory nature of Judaism and Christ's fulfillment of prophecy), the *Chronicle* (which demonstrates the antiquity of the Jews), and *On the Theophany* (which considers the transcendence of God in the flesh and depends on the *D.E.*), also make use of Josephan material. It should be kept in mind that although there are considerable differences among the various works, they document the *Heilsgeschichte* in which the divine salvation is worked out from Judaism, whose roots extend far back into antiquity, through the death and resurrection of Jesus, to the triumph of the Church.

In the *Demonstration of the Gospel* Eusebius recounts the Hasmonean ascendency to the high priesthood and the restoration of the title of king which was lost with the Babylonian captivity. Eusebius mentions that, according to Josephus, Jonathan became high priest (*A.J.* 20.238; *D.E.* 8.2.394 [380, 26]) and Aristobulus was the first since the exile to "put on the royal diadem" (*A.J.* 13.301; *D.E.* 8.2.394 [380, 28f.]).[12]

Herod the Great is accorded considerable attention in the *Ecclesiastical History*, since it was during his reign that the prophecy, "A ruler will not fail from Judah nor a leader from his loins until he comes for whom it is reserved" (Gen 49:10),[13] began to be fulfilled (*H.E.* 1.6.1 [48, 4ff.]). Thus the

---

[12] *D.E.:* ⁻ὃς πρῶτος ... διάδημα βασιλικὸν περιτίθεται. *A.J.:* διάδημα πρῶτος ἐπιτίθεται (coni. Niese: περιτίθεται).
[13] οὐκ ἐκλείψειν ἄρχοντα ἐξ Ἰούδα οὐδὲ ἡγούμενον ἐκ τῶν μηρῶν αὐτοῦ ... ἕως ἂν ἔλθῃ ᾧ ἀπόκεται.

fascination with Herod is a function of Eusebius' preoccupation with Christ who was born at the end of his reign. Eusebius notes that Herod's father was Idumean while his mother was an Arab (*H.E.* 1.6.2 [48, 11f.] alluding to *B.J.* 1.123, 181 and/or *A.J.* 14.8f., 121).

Eusebius notes that Josephus informs us of Herod's practice of appointing priests not of the old priestly order (Josephus states that Herod appointed individuals not of the Hasmonean family) and of locking up the high priest's vestments (*A.J.* 18.92-93 and 20.247-249; *H.E.* 1.6.9-10 [52, 1-11] is a summary of Josephan material; *D.E.* 8.2.93-96 [384, 25-385, 16] is a citation derived from Julius Africanus[14]). Josephus indicates that this was a safeguard by Herod against any possible revolt, a practice which was perpetuated by his successors; for Eusebius, on the other hand, Herod's behavior was fulfillment of biblical prophecy. Eusebius interpreted the time after the seventy weeks of Daniel 9:24-27 as including the cessation of the anointing of high priests. As the traditional high priestly succession came to an end through Herod's habit of appointing individuals of questionable lineage and as Christ was born during Herod's reign, Josephus provides a historical witness to the priesthood of Christ promised by Scripture. Atonement for sin which was the provenance of the properly anointed high priest was thereby transferred to Christ, God's anointed high priest. It is interesting that Eusebius sees the "legitimate" high priesthood coming to an end with Herod rather than earlier with the Hasmonean accession to the high priesthood by Simon. We cannot expect Josephus, given his claim to priestly status as well as to Hasmonean lineage, to have any doubts about the legitimacy or authority of the Hasmonean high priests.

According to Eusebius, Herod's end was grim in repayment for the deaths of the innocents in Bethlehem and its environs (Matt 2:16). The Gospel does not mention the nature of Herod's demise but, for the bishop, Josephus' account indicates divine retribution for the king's cruel deed. Eusebius cites Josephus' account of Herod's last illness (*A.J.* 17.168-170 in *H.E.* 1.8.5-8 [64, 26-66, 12])[15] which describes the physical aspects of Herod's malady: ulceration of the colon, inflammation in the bladder, worms and difficulty in breathing. Eusebius continues by citing a passage which he thinks to be from the second book of the *Jewish War* but actually is *B.J.* 1. 656-660 (*H.E.* 1.8.9-14 [66, 16-68, 23][16]): Herod, hoping to find a cure, went to bathe at Callirrhoe, located above Lake

---

[14] T. Gaisford, ed., *Eclogai Prophetetica in* Eusebii Pamphili *(Paris, 1857)*, P G 22.1135 and 1138. Eusebius is probably citing Julius Africanus who himself is citing Josephus. The text of Josephus cited by Africanus is essentially the same as what we find in the *D.E.* Both passages share common differences from Niese's text of *A.J.* 18.92-93. Therefore, it is most likely that Eusebius is citing Josephus through Julius Africanus.

[15] For a comparative analysis of these texts, see Schwartz, clxxxii ff. They show that the original Eusebian text underwent considerable correction.

[16] Schwartz, clxxv.

Asphaltitus (the Dead Sea) to no avail. He returned thereupon to Jericho where
he decided to have certain captives executed upon his own death lest the Jews
celebrate his demise. Eusebius continues (*H.E.* 1.8.14 [70, 2-6] citing *B.J.* I,
662) by relating that Herod took a knife ostensibly to peel an apple and
attempted suicide. Finally, the historian, paraphrasing Josephus, mentions that
on his deathbed Herod ordered the execution of another son after having two
others killed (*H.E.* 1.8.15-16 [70, 7-16]; cf. *A.J.* 17.187, 191 and *B.J.* 1.664,
665). Eusebius closes his account of Herod's life and death with this summary:
"He paid a just penalty on account of the children he murdered at Bethlehem for
the sake of his plot against our savior" (*H.E.* 1.8.16 [70, 11-13]).[17]

Eusebius narrates Augustus' disposition of Herod's kingdom among his
various sons. He uses Josephus to corroborate his account of Archelaus'
accession to the throne and his fall after ten years, Philip's inheritance of
Trachonitis and Herod Antipas' possession of his tetrarchy (*H.E.* 1.9.1 [70, 20-
72, 2]; *A.J.* 17.317-319, 342-344).[18] Eusebius, however, is unclear whether he
is still following Josephus when he mentions the name of Lysanius, tetrarch of
Abilene, in his list. In all probability Eusebius is thinking of Luke 3:1 which
also lists Herod (Antipas), Philip, Lysanias and their respective territories.
Lysanias' name really does not belong in a list of Herod's sons but his name is
linked with those of Philip and Antipas in Luke and thus finds its way into the
Ecclesiastical History.

The Census of Luke 2 is considered in the *Ecclesiastical History* (1.5).
Eusebius cites *A.J.* 18.1 (*H.E.* 1.5.4 [46, 6-10]) on the appointment of
Quirinius to the governship of Syria and his commission to conduct a census of
Judea. He continues by quoting *A.J.* 18.4 (*H.E.* 1.5.5 [46, 12-15]) on the
ensuing rebellion by Judas the Gaulanite. Eusebius then turns to *B.J.* 2.118
(*H.E.* 1.5.6 [46, 18-20]) on Judas' incitement of the Galilee to rebellion against
the Romans.

Eusebius employs Josephus to explain a problem with Luke 3:2: "In the
high-priesthood of Annas and Caiaphas, the word of God came upon John son of
Zechariah in the desert."[19] Luke's text could be read as stating that both Annas
and Caiaphas were high priests simultaneously. The historian recognizes that
this is an impossibility and cites Josephus to show that Caiaphas eventually
succeeded Annas in the office (*A.J.* 18.34-35 in *H.E.* 1.10.4-5 [74, 10-16]; also
D.E. 8.2.399 [386, 4-10]). Eusebius notes that John's activity spanned the time
from Annas' high priesthood until Caiaphas held the office. The entire time

---

[17] ποινὴν δικαίαν ἐκτίσαντος ὧν ἀμφὶ τὴν Βηθλεὲμ ἀνεῖλεν παίδων τῆς τοῦ
σωτῆρος ἡμῶν ἐπιβουλῆς ἕνεκα·

[18] *B.J.* 1.668-669 and 2.93-94, 211 parallel much of the information in the *A.J.*
However, in the *B.J.* Archelaus' reign ended in the ninth year and not in the tenth
as we find in the *A.J.* 17 and the *H.E.*

[19] ἐπὶ ἀρχιερέως Ἅννα καὶ Καϊάφα, ἐγένετο ῥῆμα θεοῦ ἐπὶ Ἰωάννην τὸν
Ζαχαρίου υἱὸν ἐν τῇ ἐρήμῳ.

from Annas to Caiaphus could not, according to the information provided by Josephus, have been more than four years. In that Caiaphus was high priest at the time of the Passion, Josephus' provides a time-frame compatible with Eusebius' reading of the Gospels.

The story of John the Baptist as recorded in the Gospels receives confirmation of sorts from Josephus' narrative on Herod Antipas, Herodias and the death of John (*H.E.* 1.11.1ff. [76, 9ff.]; cf. *A.J.* 8.109ff.). Eusebius informs his readers of Josephus' explanation that John the Baptist was beheaded by Herod Antipas who had divorced his spouse, the daughter of Aretas the king of the Petraeans, and had married his brother's wife, Herodias. The slight paid to his daughter compelled Aretas to wage war with Antipas whose entire army was lost to the Petraeans. Eusebius avoids the problem posed by Mark and Matthew with regard to the former husband of Herodias. Both Gospels identify Herodias' husband as Philip (Mark 6:17 and Matt 14:3).[20] Luke, however, merely refers to Herodias as his brother's wife (Luke 3:19).[21] Eusebius summarizes the text of *Antiquities* and avoids Josephus' protracted discussion of Antipas' trip to Rome, where he met Herodias, and details of the war with his father-in-law, Aretas. The historian notes Herodias' responsibility for Antipas' eventual fall (the manner of which is not discussed) and his banishment to Vienne in Gaul. He states that his defeat by the army of Aretas was a divine chastisement for his murder of John.

Josephus, according to Eusebius, describes John as "particularly righteous" (μάλιστα δικαιότατον) and in the eighteenth book of the *Antiquities* he writes:

> Now to some of the Jews it appeared that the army of Herod had been destroyed by God and that he was paying a just penalty for John called the Baptist. For Herod killed him, a good man, who commanded the Jews, cultivating virtue to practice righteousness toward one another and piety toward God, coming together in baptism: for baptism would prove acceptable to him only for those who did not use it to escape sins but for purity of the body, on condition that the soul had been cleansed by righteousness. And when the others gathered together, for they were greatly excited at the hearing of his words, Herod feared his considerable persuasiveness among men, lest they lead to a revolt for it looked like they would do his counsel. He thought it much better to kill him in anticipation before a revolution should come from him, rather than regret

---

[20] The identity of Philip as the husband of Herodias is omitted in Codex D (and the Italic texts). As this western ms generally betrays more expansive readings than the more important Alexandrian mss, this variant suggests a correction to the reading originally taken from Mark. However, what did the redactor correct from: Luke or possibly Josephus?

[21] Could Luke have noted Mark's error and corrected it from Josephus? See M. Krenkel, *Josephus und Lukas* (Leipzig,1894). Although Krenkel's thesis, that Luke employed Josephan material for both the Gospel and Acts, has fallen into neglect, passages such as Luke 3:19 are provocative.

becoming embroiled in matters coming about violently. Through Herod's suspicion he was sent as a captive to Macherus, the prison already mentioned, and there was put to death. (*H.E.* 1.11.4-6 [78, 1-16]; cf. *A.J.* 18.116-119)[22]

This passage on John in the *Ecclesiastical History* is cited in part in the *Demonstration of the Gospel* (*D.E.* 9.5.15 [416, 17-23]; cf. *A.J.* 18.116-117).[23] Two elements are of particular interest: First, passage reflects a positive view of John. He is described as a righteous man whose unjust fate was decreed by Herod Antipas owing to the latter's fear of the masses. Second, Antipas feared sedition incited by this man and therefore did away with him lest John threaten his political security. That John could be treated positively by Josephus does not require a great stretch of the imagination. It is of course possible that our text of the *Antiquities* underwent some Christian emendation but the claim made by the Gospels for John, that he was the forerunner of Christ, is not made. This is not a passage such as the *Testimonium Flavianum* where the writer sounds like the Christian he was not. To Josephus, John was a holy ascetic put to death by a petty oriental despot who feared for his security. What is noteworthy is that Josephus explains the reason for John's execution differently than do the Gospels. All three Gospels see John's death as punishment for his condemnation of Herod's adultery for having taken his brother's wife. Matthew follows Mark in explaining how at Herod's birthday the daughter of Herodias extracted a vow to grant her whatsoever she wished after dancing for him. The wish was, of course, John's head. Josephus does not record this incident nor does he place the blame for John's death on Herodias and her daughter. The Herod Antipas of Mark and Matthew is a weak-willed creature who is manipulated by women in his household to do an abhorrent deed. The Antipas of Josephus is a despot who executes a charismatic religious leader whom he fears might endanger the security of his realm and thereby bring about Roman displeasure and his own fall. What is amazing is that Eusebius does not appear to see the difference. Eusebius focuses on Josephus' portrayal of the righteous

---

[22] τισὶ δὲ τῶν Ἰουδαίων ἐδόκει ὀλωλέναι τὸν Ἡρώδου στρατὸν ὑπὸ τοῦ θεοῦ, καὶ μάλα δικαίως τιννυμένου κατὰ ποινὴν Ἰωάννου τοῦ καλουμένου βαπτιστοῦ. κτείνει γὰρ τοῦτον Ἡρώδης, ἀγαθὸν ἄνδρα καὶ τοῖς ' Ἰουδαίος κελεύοντα ἀρετὴν ἐπασκοῦσιν καὶ τὰ πρὸς ἀλλήλους δικαιοσύνῃ καὶ πρὸς τὸν θεὸν εὐσεβείᾳ χρωμένους βαπτισμῷ συνιέναι· οὕτω γὰρ δὴ καὶ τὴν βάπτισιν ἀποδεκτὴν αὐτῷ φανεῖσθαι, μὴ ἐπὶ τινων ἁμαρτάδων παραιτήσει χρωμένων, ἀλλ ἐφ' ἁγείᾳ τοῦ σώματος, ἅτε δὴ καὶ τῆς ψυχῆς δικαιοσύνῃ προεκκεκαθαρμένης. καὶ τῶν ἄλλων συστρεφομένων (καὶ γὰρ ἤρθησαν ἐπὶ πλεῖστον τῇ ἀκροάσει τῶν λόγων), δείσας Ἡρώδης τὸ ἐπὶ τοσόνδε πιθανὸν αὐτοῦ τοῖς ἀνθρώποις, μὴ ἐπὶ ἀποστάσει τινὶ φέροι (πάντα γὰρ ἐοίκεσαν συμβουλῇ τῇ ἐκείνου πράξοντες), πολὺ κρεῖττον ἡγεῖται, πρίν τι νεώτερον ὑπ' αὐτοῦ γενέσθαι, προλαβὼν ἀναιρεῖν, ἢ μεταβολῆς γενομένης εἰς πράγματα ἐμπεσὼν μετανοεῖν. καὶ ὁ μὲν ὑποψίᾳ τῇ Ἡρώδης δέσμιος εἰς τὸν Μαχαιροῦντα πεμφθείς, τὸ προειρημένον φρούριον, ταύτῃ κρίνυται.

[23] The only significant difference between the text of the *D.E.* and that of the *H.E.* (and *A.J.*) is that we find τὸν Ἰουδαίων στρατὸν instead of τὸν Ἡρώδης στρατὸν.

Baptist done in by Herod whose fall from power is occasioned by his wife Herodias. Her goading of Antipas into seeking the title of king from Caesar ultimately leads to his banishment (*A.J.* 18.240-255). The role played by Herodias in Herod's banishment is important to Eusebius because it is congruent with the Gospels' portrait of her as a manipulating wife. This element of Josephus' narrative seemed then to confirm the Gospels' account of John's death.

In Book 2 of the *Ecclesiastical History*, Eusebius traces history of the Jews from the beginning of the period treated in the Acts of the Apostles to the beginning of the Jewish War. The historian interweaves material from Acts with that of Clement, Tertullian, Josephus and Philo (*H.E.* 2.table of contents [100, 19-20]).

Eusebius pays attention to the history of the Roman emperors for it was through the agency of Gaius (Caligula) that Agrippa II received the throne, not only of his uncle Philip but also of Lysanius and his uncle Herod Antipas who was banished along with his wife Herodias (*H.E.* 2.4.1 [114, 13-20]; cf. *B.J.* 2.180; *A.J.* 18.224-225, 237, 252 and 255). Eusebius notes that this Herod was (Antipas) that of the Passion (a detail which did not come from Josephus).

Philo is of interest to Eusebius for he recorded the tragedies which befell his people because, in Eusebius' words, "of the crimes of the Jews against Christ" (*H.E.* 2.5.6 [118, 11]).[24] The historian cites *A.J.* 18.257-260 regarding Philo's presence among the Jewish embassy to Emperor Gaius (Caligula) following civil disturbances between the Jews and Greeks in Alexandria. We now arrive at a theme which will be developed more fully in Eusebius' treatment of the Jewish War: The misfortunes of the Jewish people and the destruction of the Jewish nation are a result of their rejection of Christ and the crucifixion. It is important to note a significant difference between Josephus and Eusebius regarding the events which preceded the war: Josephus is offering an explanation of the war's causes. His narrative draws a portrait of bad government and events which would lead to the triumph of Judean extremists and the resulting destructive war. Eusebius derives many details from Josephus but does not share his purpose. To the Christian historian, the reasons for the war are not as important as the prophecies in the Gospels which predicted it. Eusebius draws scenes from the Jewish historian which provide background material on events and persons relevant to the New Testament or which serve his thesis that the events to come were predicted by Christ. Eusebius appears insensitive to the developing tragedy narrated by Josephus for he has replaced human drama with the relentless unfolding of prophecy.

The case of Pontius Pilate is a typical example of the aforementioned divergence in purpose between Josephus and Eusebius. Josephus' portrait of Pilate exemplifies the sort of bad government which would inflame the Jews to revolt. For Eusebius, Pilate figures as a central character in the Passion of

---

24 τῶν κατὰ τοῦ Χριστοῦ τετολημένων ἕνεκεν Ἰουδαίοις συμβεβηκότων.

Christ, a Jewish crime against Jesus (*H.E.* 2.6.3 [120, 14]). It is noteworthy that Eusebius follows Josephus in portraying Pilate as a reprehensible figure. This is not the case with the Gospels which avoid judgments of the procurator and, indeed, fail to assign him blame for the death of Jesus. As with his treatment of Herod Antipas, Eusebius does not distinguish here between Josephus' depiction of Pilate and that of the evangelists. Eusebius cites Josephus' account of the affair of the standards as paradigmatic of the procurator's behavior:

> Pilate, having been sent by Tiberias to Judaea as procurator, having brought by night into Jerusalem images of Caesar, called standards, covered [them] up. When day came, the greatest tumult arose among the Jews. For they were astounded by what was near in sight, since their laws were being trampled on. For they do not permit any image to be set up in the city. (*H.E.* 2.6.4 [120, 18-23]; cf. *B.J.* 2.169-170)[25]

Eusebius treats this subject not only in the *Ecclesiastical History* but also in the *Demonstration of the Gospel* 8.2.122 (390, 1-5, apparently referring to *A.J.* 18.55-56)[26] and in the *Chronicle* (Jerome) 175, 11-24. These latter differ from the text as cited in the *Ecclesiastical History* in an important detail: the standards are not brought into the city but into the Temple area.[27] *D.E.* 8.2.123 (390, 5) notes that Philo (evidently in a lost work) confirms the data drawn from Josephus.[28] Perhaps Eusebius has embellished Josephan material with a tradition recorded by Philo or cites the *Antiquities* passage indirectly from another source, such as we have seen with Julius Africanus. We can say nothing more than that Eusebius utilized *B.J.* 2 in writing the section on Pilate in his *Ecclesiastical History* while in the preparation of the *Chronicle* and the *Preparation of the Gospel* (the latter probably using *A.J.* 18), he ascribes to Josephus a tradition belonging to Philo. A final possiblity is that the bishop made use of an unknown source which contaminates the Josephan material.

Eusebius' description of Pilate's reprehensible character continues with the citation of Josephus' account of Pilate's appropriation of the *Corban* to build an aqueduct and the violent means used by Pilate to contain the ensuing protest (*B.J.* 2.175-177 in *H.E.* 2.6.6-7 [122,4-11]). The historian concludes by noting that Josephus documents other revolts and continuous turmoil from this time

---

[25] πεμφθεὶς δὲ εἰς 'Ιουδαίαν ἐπίτροπος ὑπὸ Τιβερίου Πιλᾶτος νύκτωρ κεκαλυμμένας εἰς 'Ιεροσόλυμα παρεισκομίζει τὰς Καίσαρος εἰκόνας σημαῖαι καλοῦνται. τοῦτο μεθ' ἡμέραν μεγίστην ταραχὴν ἤγειρεν τοῖς 'Ιουδαίοις. οἵ τε γὰρ ἐγγὺς πρὸς τὴν ὄψιν ἐξεπλάγησαν, ὡς πεπατημένων αὐτοῖς τῶν νόμων· οὐδὲν γὰρ ἀξιοῦσιν ἐν τῇ πόλει δείκηλον τίθεσθαι.

[26] *A.J.* 18.55 refers to Pilate as Πιλᾶτος δὲ ὁ τῆς 'Ιουδαίας ἡγεμὼν στρατιὰν (as opposed to ἐπίτροπος . . . Πιλᾶτος in *B.J.* 2.169). In the *D.E.* Eusebius follows *A.J.* by referring to Pilate as Πιλᾶτον τὸν ἡγεμόνα.

[27] *D.E.* VIII, 2, 122 (390, 3): εἰς τὸ ἱερον and *Chron.* (Jerome) 175, 21: *in templo.*

[28] αὐτὰ δὴ ταῦτα καὶ ὁ Φίλων συμμαρτυρεῖ.

down to the ultimate siege of Jerusalem by Vespasian. To this he appends his own interpretation of these events: "The judgment of God thus pursued the Jews on account of their crimes against Christ" (*H.E.* 2.6.8 [122, 20-22]).[29]

Eusebius, noting the famine described in Acts 11, mentions that this occurred during the reign of Claudius who had succeeded Gaius after less than four years (*H.E.* 2.8.1 [124, 3-4]). In that this information follows in the *Jewish War* close after the material on Pilate (*B.J.* 2.204; v. also *A.J.* 19.201), it may derive from Josephus.

Herod Agrippa's role in the death of James and the arrest of Peter is the subject of Acts 12. Eusebius, citing Acts 12:19, 21-23, describes the events surrounding Agrippa's death: after making an oration, he is hailed as a god by the people of Tyre and Sidon. As he does not refuse the acclamation, he is struck down by an angel of God, consumed with worms and dies. The historian cites at length the account of Agrippa's death in the *Antiquities* (*A.J.* 343-351 in *H.E.* 2.10.1-9 [126, 20-130, 10]) with an important exception: It is not the presence of an owl which is the harbinger of his doom (*A.J.* 19.346; cf. *A.J.* 18.195) but an angel (*H.E.* 2.10.6 [128, 9-10]).[30] We see for the first time a conscious alteration of the Josephan text to make it serve Eusebius' purpose: the testimony of Josephus confirms the accuracy of the New Testament. On the other hand, a discrepancy between Acts and the *Antiquities* either unnoticed or deemed unimportant by Eusebius is that, according to Josephus, Agrippa is not acclaimed a god by the masses following an oration but because of his silver robe which glistened in the sun (*A.J.* 19.344-345 in *H.E.* 2.10.4-5 [126, 25-128, 8]).

The author of Acts 5:34-39 has the Pharisee Gamaliel speak out to save Peter and the other apostles whom the council wishes to have killed. He counsels caution lest they be found opposing God if they persecute these men. Gamaliel reminds his audience that pernicious elements in Judean society had come and gone, among them Theudas and Judas the Galilean whose rebellion occurred at the time of the census. The speech makes a critical error in antedating Theudas. The literature is abundant regarding this chronological error and the possible relationship between Luke-Acts and Josephus.[31] Eusebius

---

[29] Ἰουδαίους μὲν οὖν ὧν κατὰ τοῦ Χριστοῦ τετολμήκασιν, ταύτῃ πῃ τὰ ἐκ τῆς θείας μετῄει δίκης˙

[30] *A.J.* 19.346: ἀνακύψας δ οὖν μετ ὀλίγον τὸν βουβῶνα τῆς ἑαυτοῦ κεφαλῆς ὑπερκαθιζόμενον εἶδεν ἐπὶ σχοινίου τινός ("But shortly after, looking up he saw an owl perched on a rope above his head.") *H.E.* II, 10, 6 (128, 9-10): ἀνακύψας δ᾽ οὖν μετ ὀλίγον, τῆς ἑαυτοῦ κεφαλῆς ὑπερκαθιζόμενον εἶδεν ἄγγελον ("But shortly after, looking up he saw an angel perched above his head.")

[31] If Krenkel's thesis (*Josephus und Lukas* [Leipzig,1894]) is correct, Luke erred in reading *A.J.* 20.102 which mentions the death of the sons of Judas the Galilean who rebelled at the time of the census. Luke crafted Gamaliel's speech following Josephus' order, which was chronological, but missing the point that Josephus was discussing the sons of Judas and not the father. Therefore, Gamaliel's speech

wants to use Josephus as witness to the accuracy of Acts but he has noted the discrepancy. Unlike the account of Agrippa's death, he cannot correct it by altering a few words. His recourse is to cite *A.J.* 20.97-98 on the rising of Theudas during the procuratorship of Fadus without mentioning Josephus' information on Judas the Galilean (*H.E.* 2.11.2-3 [130, 24-132, 3]), which he cannot without contradicting his assertion than Josephus confirms the New Testament.

Eusebius continues to parallel the *Antiquities* and Acts by citing *A.J.* 20.101 on Queen Helena's relief of the famine in Judea. According to Eusebius, this confirms Acts 11 regarding the famine relief carried out by Barnabus and Paul (*H.E.* 2.11.3-2.12.2 [132, 4-13]).

The next subject dealt with by Eusebius is the death of James, brother of Jesus. He cites a reading not extant in our texts: "These things happened to the Jews as revenge for James the Just, who was the brother of Jesus called the Christ, for the Jews killed him despite his great righteousness" (*H.E.* 2.23.20 [172, 9-11]).[32] It would seem reasonable that these lines belong with *A.J.* 20.197, 199-203 which Eusebius quotes (*H.E.* 2.23.21-24 [172, 14-174, 11]).[33] The text of *Antiquities* relates how the high priest Ananus convened a sanhedrin to try "the brother of the one called Christ, a man named James and certain others" (*A.J.* 20.200)[34] who were unjustly condemned and stoned. It is Eusebius, and not our text of *Antiquities*, which informs us of the sobriquet "the Just" and it is the Christian who connects James' death with the destruction of Jerusalem in the war. Eusebius could be guilty of attributing to Josephus words of his own composition although it is just as likely that he is actually reproducing what he considers genuinely Josephan. We have seen Eusebius alter

---

contains a chronological error. It has been suggested that Luke possessed a source independent of Josephus (see C. C. Torrey, *The Composition and Date of Acts* [1916], 71 and H. St. J. Thackeray, *Selections from Josephus* [1919], 194) given Luke's statement that Theudas had 400 followers (a fact not related by Josephus).

[32] ταῦτα δὲ συμβέβηκεν ᾽Ιουδαίοις κατ᾽ ἐκδίκησιν ᾽Ιακώβου τοῦ δικαίου, ὃς ἦν ἀδελφὸς ᾽Ιησοῦ τοῦ λεγομένου Χριστοῦ, ἐπειδήπερ δικαιόντατον αὐτὸν ὄντα οἱ ᾽Ιουδαῖοι ἀπέκτειναν.

[33] With regard to the genuineness of *A.J.* 20.200-201, there is nothing which would cause us to reject it as spurious. Despite Origen's surprise that Josephus should be sensitive to the unjustness of James' fate given that he was not a Christian (*Com. in Mt.* 10.17), there is nothing to mark the passage as a Christian interpolation. If the passage were of Christan origin, no doubt more would have been made of James or Jesus, "called the Christ." See Paul Winter, "Excursus II--Josephus on Jesus and James *Ant.* xviii, 3, 3 (63-4) and xx 9, 1 (200-3)," in E. Schürer's *The History of the Jewish People in the Age of Jesus Christ*, eds. G. Vermes, F. Millar and M. Black (Edinburgh, 1973), 1:428-441, especially 431-432.

[34] τὸν ἀδελφὸν ᾽Ιησοῦ τοῦ λεγομένου Χριστοῦ, ᾽Ιάκωβος ὄνομα αὐτῷ, καὶ τινας ἑτέρους.

a reading regarding the death of Herod Agrippa, but this is quite different from creating a text in its entirety. Eusebius could be citing Josephus through a secondary source which contained theological comments on the text[35] or he might be using a text which some Christian scribe has emended. As we shall see, Eusebius' text included the *Testimonium Flavianum*, which betrays a Christian hand, and the otherwise unknown citation may have been such an emendation. Although the source of the scribal emendation would be unknown, it should be remembered that although Origen attributes to Josephus his notion of Jerusalem's destruction as retribution for James' death (*C. Cels.* 2.13), he does not offer a citation. Given Eusebius' proclivity for Origen's theology and Origen's own association with Caesaria, perhaps the citation had its source in literature of that theological circle. Origen, however, was not the sole Christian writer who drew a connection between the death of James and the destruction of Jerusalem. Eusebius cites Hegesippus' narrative on the death of James and notes that Vespasian besieged the city immediately upon the death of James (*H.E.* 2.23.18 [170, 23-24]).[36] It would be naive to assume that Hegesippus is concerned merely with chronology. Hegesippus, Origen and the passage Eusebius attributes to Josephus may be traces of an otherwise lost tradition regarding James the Just and the destruction of Jerusalem. Despite the citations, Eusebius differs from Origen and Hegesippus in ascribing the cause of destruction of Jerusalem to the death of Jesus rather than to the stoning of James the Just.

After treating James, Eusebius turns to Jesus himself and cites what is certainly the most problematic of Josephan texts:

> At his time Jesus arose, a wise man, if indeed he must be called a man, for he was a doer of marvelous deeds, a teacher of men who received the truth with pleasure (*D.E.*: "honored the truth") and he led many of the Jews and many of the Gentiles. This one was the Christ and when Pilate sentenced him to the cross at the instigation of leading men among us, those who first loved him did not stop for after three days buried he appeared to them alive, and the divine prophets told these and ten thousand other wonders (*D.E.* omits "wonders") about him. And up to now the tribe of Christians named after him has not failed.[37] (*H.E.*

---

[35] suggested by H. Schreckenberg, *Die Flavius-Josephus-Tradition in Antike und Mittelalter* (Leiden,1972), 86.

[36] μάρτυς οὗτος ἀληθὴς 'Ιουδαῖος τε καὶ "Ελλησιν γεγένηται ὅτι 'Ιησοῦς ὁ Χριστός ἐστιν. καὶ εὐθὺς Οὐεσπασιανὸς πολιορκεῖ αὐτούς. "He became a true witness both to the Jews and to the Greeks that Jesus is the Christ. And immediately Vespasian besieged them."

[37] *H.E.*: γίνεται δὲ κατὰ τοῦτον τὸν χρόνον 'Ιησοῦς, σοφὸς ἀνήρ, εἴ γε ἄνδρα αὐτὸν λέγειν χρή. ἦν γὰρ παραδόξων ἔργων ποιητής, διδάσκαλος ἀνθρώπων τῶν ἡδονῇ τἀληθῆ δεχομένων, καὶ πολλοὺς μὲν τῶν 'Ιουδαίων, πολλοὺς δὲ καὶ ἀπὸ τοῦ 'Ελληνικοῦ ἐπηγάγετο. ὁ Χριστὸς οὗτος ἦν, καὶ αὐτὸν ἐνδείξει τῶν πρώτων ἀνδρῶν παρ᾽ ἡμῖν σταυρῷ ἐπιτετιμηκότος Πιλάτου, οὐκ ἐπαύσαντο οἱ τὸ πρῶτον ἀγ'απήσαντες ἐφάνη γὰρ αὐτοῖς

1.11.7-8 [78, 19-80, 9]; *D.E.* 3.5. 105-106 [130, 17-131, 2]; *Theo.* 250.10-20 citing *A.J.* 18.63-64)

This passage from *Antiquities* is surrounded by conjecture. Although we do not possess a ms of *Antiquities* which does not contain it, serious doubts as to its Josephan origin have been raised. The literature on this subject is vast and is of no real significance to our purpose here except to note that Eusebius is the first Christian to cite this supposedly Josephan passage.[38] Origen, as previously noted, asserted that Josephus did not believe in Jesus' messiahship (*Comm. in Matthaeum* 10:17) which the *Testimonium Flavianum*, if genuinely Josephan, clearly indicates. However, we must note that while Eusebius cites the passage, he designates the author simply as "a historian from the Hebrews themselves"[39] (*H.E.* 1.12.1 [80, 15]) and not as a Christian. Although this would seem to contradict the argument that Origen could not have known of the *Testimonium Flavianum* because of his statement regarding Josephus, it is obvious that Eusebius needs Josephus to be a Jew. Eusebius' contention is that Josephus, who is a known Jewish historian, supports the testimony of the New Testament regarding John the Baptist and Jesus:

> When a historian from the Hebrews themselves transmitted these things regarding John the Baptist and our Savior in his own writing, what alternative is there left but to thoroughly refute those shameless ones who have invented the reports about them? (*H.E.* 1.11.9 [80, 10-13])[40]

τρίτην ἔχων ἡμέραν πάλιν ζῶν, τῶν θείων προφητῶν ταῦτά τε καὶ ἄλλα μυρία περὶ αὐτοῦ θαυμάσια εἰρηκότων. εἰς ἔτι τε νῦν τῶν Χριστιανῶν ἀπὸ τοῦδε ὠνομασμένων οὐκ ἐπέλιπε τὸ φῦλον.

H.E		*D.E.*	
78,19	κατὰ τοῦτον	130, 17	κατ᾿ ἐκεῖνον
80, 2	τῶν ἡδονῇ	130, 19	omitted
80, 2	δεχομένων	130, 19	σεβομένων
80, 3	Ἰουδαίων	130, 19	Ἰουδαϊκοῦ
80, 4	τῶν πρώτων ἀνδρῶν	130, 21	τῶν παρ᾿ ἡμῖν παρ᾿ ἡμῖν ἀρχόντων
80, 6	τρίτην ἔχων ἡμέραν	130, 23	τρίτην ἡμέραν
80,7	θαυμάσια	131, 1	omitted
80, 8	εἰς ἔτι τε νῦν τῶν	131, 1	ὅθεν εἰσέτι νῦν dπὸ Χριστιανῶν ἀπὸ τοῦδε οὐδε τῶν Χριστιανῶν
80, 9	ἐπέλιπε	131, 2	ἐπέλειπεν

The Syriac *Theophany* tends to support the *Ecclesiastical History*.

[38] Recent and rather complete bibliographies of the scholarship on the *Testimonium Flavianum* are found in Winter, *op. cit.*, and Feldman, *op. cit.*

[39] τοῦ ἐξ αὐτῶν Ἑβραίων συγγραφέως.

[40] ταῦτα τοῦ ἐξ αὐτῶν Ἑβραίων συγγραφέως ἀνέκαθεν τῇ ἑαυτοῦ γραφῇ περί τε τοῦ βαπτιστοῦ Ἰωάννου καὶ τοῦ σωτῆρους ἡμῶν παραδεδωκότως, τίς ἂν ἔτι λείποιτο ἀποφυγὴ τοῦ μὴ ἀναισχύντους ἀπελέγχεσθαι τοὺς τὰ κατ᾿ αὐτῶν πλασαμένους ὑπομνήματα;

Eusebius sees Josephus' Jewishness as proof of the Christian claims for Jesus' messiahship. Josephus was both a noted historian and a Jew, thus aware of matters concerning the Jewish people and history in his century. That no one reading the *Testimonium Flavianum* could help but recognize a Christian hand would not occur to Eusebius who regarded Josephus as a Jewish witness to the veracity of the New Testament.

Books II and III of the *Ecclesiastical History* continue to trace people and events from the Ascension of Christ to the Jewish war (*H.E.* 2. preface.2 [102, 7-10]). Eusebius utilizes Josephus along with others, particularly Philo, Clement, and Tertullian (*H.E..* 2.table of contents [100, 19-20]), to complement primarily the Acts of the Apostles. As we have already seen, Josephus must confirm the accuracy of the New Testament.

Paul's meeting with Aquila and Priscilla in Corinth after their banishment from Rome due to Claudius' edict (Acts 18:1-3) prompts Eusebius to refer to Josephus' account of riots in Jerusalem at Passover during the reign of Claudius and the resulting deaths of thirty thousand persons. Following the riots, Claudius sent Agrippa as king and appointed Felix as procurator of Samaria, Galilee and Peraea (*H.E.* 2.19.1-2 [158, 1-12]; cf. *B.J.* 2.227, 247-248).

Eusebius cites *Antiquities* 20.180-181 (*H.E.* 2.20.1-3 [158, 16-26]) on the violence among the priests in Jerusalem and summarizes Josephus' description of the Sicarii's nefarious activities (*B.J.* 2.254-256 in *H.E.* 2.20.4-6 [158, 27-160, 9]). The Egyptian false prophet is the subject of a citation from the *Jewish War* 2.261-263 (*H.E.* 2.21.1-2 [160, 11-21]).[41] What ties all three passages together is that they relate to the Acts of the Apostles. The violence among the priests and the rise of the Sicarii occurred during the procuratorship of Felix, a figure known in Acts. Finally, the Egyptian prophet is mentioned in Acts 21:38. For Eusebius, the history of the early Church narrated in Acts is paralleled by Josephus' account of the events which led to the Jewish War. Eusebius draws from the latter when there is some contact with the former.

The *Ecclesiastical History* now turns to the beginning of the Jewish War. Eusebius summarizes how, under the procurator Florus many thousands in Jerusalem were tortured and perished in the twelfth year of Nero's reign (*B.J.* 2.284, 306-308[42] in *H.E.* 2.26.1 [178, 16-21]). The Jews of Syria were also put to the sword in retribution for their revolt in Judea (*B.J.* 2.461ff. in *H.E.* 2.26.2 [180, 1-8]) where it could be seen that

---

[41] This reference in the *Jewish War* to the false prophet or its parallel in *Antiquities* 20.169 is mentioned in the *Chronicle* (Jerome) 181.10-21.

[42] That the war began in the twelfth year of Nero's reign is also found in *A.J.* 20.257 but without the details found in the *Jewish War* and in the *Ecclesiastical History*. Eusebius indicates that he is drawing data from Josephus' detailed account of the disaster which befell the Jews (*H.E.* 2.26.1 [178, 16-17]), which would mean the *Jewish War*. Thus Eusebius probably did not make use of the *Antiquities* in this section.

"The cities were filled with unburied bodies and the corpses of the young together with the old and women stripped of any covering of their modesty. And the entire province was filled with indescribable misery, and future threats worse than present calamities." (*B.J.* 2.465 in *H.E.* 2.26.2 [180, 4-8])[43]

The *Jewish War* may have possibly provided Eusebius with two pieces of data: The *Ecclesiastical History* notes that Nero died after thirteen years on the throne (*H.E.* 3.5.1 [194, 19-20]; cf. *B.J.* 4.491)[44] and upon his ascension to the throne, Vespasian left his son Titus to prosecute the war against the Jews (*H.E.* 3.5.1 [194, 21-196, 1]; cf. *B.J.* 4.658). These historical notes preface Eusebius' description of the oracle which foretold the destruction of Jerusalem and advised the Christian community to flee to Pella. Jerusalem was to be destroyed so that "the judgement of God might finally overtake them for all their crimes against Christ and his apostles" (*H.E.* 3.5.3 [196, 20-21]).[45] Josephus' prediction that Vespasian would one day be emperor (*B.J.* 3.399ff.) is mentioned in the *Chronicle* (Jerome) 185.14-20. This prediction of Nero's death is treated by Eusebius as contemporaneous with the deaths of Peter and Paul in the first persecution of the Church by Nero.

The *Ecclesiastical History* devotes considerable space to the siege of Jerusalem and the fate of its inhabitants. As mentioned above, Eusebius was not the first to see the destruction of the city and Temple as divine punishment. Origen held that the murder of James the Just was the cause (*H.E.* 2.23.20 [172, 9-11]). Eusebius, however, views the siege of the city and the suffering of its population as divine chastisement for the death of Jesus, not James:

> Omitting the details of what happened to them by sword and other means, it is profitable to furnish only their sufferings from famine, that those who read this work might partially see how the punishment of God followed not far behind them for their outrages against the Christ of God. (*H.E.* 3.5.7 [198, 13-18])[46]

Further, Eusebius sees the plight of Jerusalem as testimony to Jesus' apocalyptic prophecies. The death of Jesus at the hands of the Jews was not a

---

[43] τὰς πόλεις μεστὰς ἀτάφων σωμάτων καὶ νεκροὺς ἅμα νηπίοις γέροντας ἐρριμμένους γύναιά τε μηδὲ τῆς ἐπ' αἰδῷ (*B.J.*: αἰδοῖ) σκέπης μετειληφότα, καὶ πᾶσαν μὲν τὴν ἐπαρχίαν μεστὴν ἀδιηγήτων συμφορῶν, μείζονα δὲ τῶν ἑκάστοτε τολμωμένων τὴν ἐπὶ τοῖς ἀπειλουμένοις ἀνάτασιν.

[44] According to *B.J.* 4.491, Nero ruled 13 years, 8 months.

[45] ἡ ἐκ θεοῦ δίκη λοιπὸν αὐτοὺς ἅτε τοσαῦτα εἴς τε τὸν Χριστὸν καὶ τοὺς ἀποστόλους αὐτοῦ παρηνομηκότας μετῄει

[46] Παρελθὼν δὴ τὰ τῶν ἐν μέρει συμβεβηκότων αὐτοῖς ὅσα διὰ ξίφους καὶ ἄλλῳ τρόπῳ κατ' αὐτῶν ἐγκεχείρηται, μόνας τὰς διὰ τοῦ λιμοῦ ἀναγκαῖον ἡγοῦμαι συμφορὰς παραθέσθαι, ὡς ἂν ἐκ μέρους ἔχοιεν οἱ τῇδε τῇ γραφῇ ἐντυγχάνοντες εἰδέναι ὅπως αὐτοὺς τῆς εἰς τὸν Χριστὸν τοῦ θεοῦ παρανομίας οὐκ εἰς μακρὸν ἡ ἐκ θεοῦ μετῆλθεν τιμωρία.

sign of failure for he had known not only of his fate but what would happen to those who had brought about his end:

> Such were the rewards for the transgressions and impieties of the Jews against the Christ. It is worthwhile to append to them the true prophecy of our Savior, in which he plainly foretold these very things: "Woe to those who are with child and give suck in those days but pray that your flight will not be in winter or on the Sabbath, for there will be then a great affliction, such as there was not from the beginning of the world until now, nor will there be." (*H.E.* 3.7.1 [210, 13-20]; citing Matt 24:19-21)[47]

The historian cites large portions of the *Jewish War* which illustrate the incredible privations of Jerusalem's populace: great wealth was exchanged for the most meagre rations while the old and very young were murdered for possession of food (*B.J.* 5.424-438 in *H.E.* 3.6.1-6, 10 [198, 21-202, 18]). The dead lay in the streets and robbers stripped the dead of their possessions. Even Titus is appalled at the sight of the dead piled in trenches outside the city walls (*B.J.* 5.512-519 in *H.E.* 3.6.11-15 [202, 20-204, 19]). Eusebius notes Josephus' own horror at the events transpiring within the city which transcended the evils of Sodom (*B.J.* 5.566 in *H.E.* 3.6.16 [204, 21-206, 2]). Starvation resulted in madness and even leather was consumed while straw was sold as food. Eusebius records Josephus' account of cannibalism in which a woman cooked and ate her infant (*B.J.* 6.193-213 in *H.E.* 3.6.17-28 [206, 4-210, 12]). Eusebius cites from the *Jewish War* without commentary, for Josephus' grisly account of Jerusalem's siege does not require embellishment. Josephus' narrative of the woman who ate her child is followed by the previously cited Matt 24:19-21, which pronounces doom upon women with their children.

Some of the same material may be found in *On the Theophany*. *B.J.* 5.442-445, regarding the criminal nature of those Jews holding the city during the siege, is cited in a Greek fragment as a fulfillment of Matt 24:21 (*Theo.* 4.21 [32, 16-22]). The Syriac *Theophany* makes use of the account of the woman's cannibalism of her infant son (*B.J.* 6.199-208) as evidence for the fulfillment of Matt 24:21 and its parallel in Luke 21:23 (*Theo.* 4.21 [198, 9-199, 17]).

Eusebius summarizes Josephus' statistical summary of the siege's conclusion: According to *B.J.* 6.426, there were 2,700,000 persons in Jerusalem during the procuratorship of Cestius. This figure excluded the lepers and otherwise levitically impure persons who could not keep the Passover feast. The

---

[47] Τοιαῦτα τῆς ᾽Ιουδαίων εἰς τὸν Χριστὸν τοῦ θεοῦ παρανομίας τε καὶ δυσσεβείας τἀπίχειρα, παραθεῖναι δ᾽ αὐτοῖς ἄξιον καὶ τὴν ἀψευδῆ τοῦ σωτῆρος ἡμῶν πρόρρησιν, δι᾽ ἧς αὐτὰ ταῦτα δηλοῖ ὧδέ πως προφητεύων ›οὐαὶ δὲ ταῖς ἐν γαστρὶ ἐχούσαις καὶ ταῖς θηλαζούσαις ἐν ἐκείναις ταῖς ἡμέραις· προσεύχεσθε δὲ ἵνα μὴ γένηται ὑμῶν ἡ φυγὴ χειμῶνος μηδὲ σαββάτῳ. ἔσται γὰρ τότε θλῖψις μεγάλη, οἵα οὐκ ἐγένετο ἀπ᾽ ἀρχῆς κόσμου ἕως τοῦ νῦν, οὐδὲ μὴ γένηται‹.

census was based on the number of Paschal lambs slaughtered assuming 10 diners for each lamb slaughtered. Eusebius rounds out Josephus' figure to 3,000,000 in *H.E.* 3.5.5 (198, 5-8). Of this population *B.J.* 6.420 places the number of prisoners at 97,000 and the dead at 1,100,000 (cf. *Chron.* [Jerome] 187, 3ff.). *H.E.* 3.7.2 (211, 20-212, 7) notes that 1,100,000 perished while those over the age of 17 were sent to Egypt (cf. *B.J.* 6.418). The tallest of the prisoners were reserved for a triumphal parade (cf. *B.J.* 6.417). In a confused summary of Josephus' account, Eusebius sets the number of prisoners aged less than 17 years at 90,000. The bishop's purpose for reciting the gruesome statistics is not left to the reader's imagination:

> These things occurred in the second year of Vespasian's reign in accordance with the prophecies of our Lord and Savior Jesus Christ, who foresaw them by divine power as if they were already present, wept for them and mourned for them according to the writing of the sacred evangelist, who appended his words. Once he expressed himself to Jerusalem herself: "If you had known, even you, in this day the things which belong to your peace but now are hid from your eyes, for the days will come upon you and your enemies will throw up ramparts around you and will encompass you, and will hem you in, and will level you and your children." [Luke 19:42-44] And then as if to the populace, "For there will be a great distress upon the earth and anger upon this people, and they will fall by the edge of the sword and be made captive among all the Gentiles and Jerusalem will be trodden by Gentiles until the times of the Gentiles be filfilled." [Luke 21:23-24] And again, "When you see Jerusalem surrounded by armies, then you will know that the desolation has drawn near." [Luke 21:20] If anyone would compare the words of our Savior with rest of the historian's narratives about the whole war, how can he not be surpised and confess how truly divine and supernaturally marvelous is the foreknowledge and foretelling of our Savior? (*H.E.* 3.7.3-6 [212, 7-214, 6][48]

---

48 ταῦτα δὲ τοῦτον ἐπράχθη τὸν τρόπον δευτέρῳ τῆς Οὐεσπασιανοῦ βασιλείας ἔτει ἀκολούθως ταῖς προγνωστικαῖς τοῦ κυρίου καὶ σωτῆρος ἡμῶν Ἰησοῦ Χριστοῦ προρρήσεσιν, θείᾳ δυνάμει ὥσπερ ἤδη παρόντα προεορακότος αὐτὰ ἐπιδακρύσαντός τε καὶ ἀποκλαυσαμένου κατὰ τὴν τῶν ἱερῶν εὐαγγελιστῶν γραφήν, οἳ καὶ αὐτὰς αὐτοῦ παρατέθεινται τὰς λέξεις, τοτὲ μὲν φήσαντος ὡς πρὸς αὐτὴν τὴν Ἰερουσαλήμ ›εἰ ἔγνως καί γε σὺ ἐν τῇ ἡμέρᾳ ταύτῃ τὰ πρὸς εἰρήνην σου· νῦν δὲ ἐκρύβη ἀπὸ ὀφθαλμῶν σου· ὅτι ἥξουσιν ἡμέραι ἐπὶ σέ, καὶ περιβαλοῦσίν σοι οἱ ἐχθροί σου χάρακα, καὶ περικυκλώσουσίν σε, καὶ συνέξουσίν σε πάντοθεν, καὶ ἐδαφιοῦσίν σε καὶ τὰ τέκνα σουκ, τοτὲ δὲ ὡς περὶ τοῦ λαοῦ ›ἔσται γὰρ ἀνάγκη μεγάλη ἐπὶ τῆς γῆς, καὶ ὀργὴ τῷ λαῷ τούτῳ καὶ πεσοῦνται ἐν στόματι μαχαίρας καὶ αἰχμαλωτισθήσονται εἰς πάντα τὰ ἔθνη καὶ Ἰερουσαλὴμ ἔσται πατουμένα ὑπὸ ἐθνῶν, ἄχρις οὗ πληρωθῶσιν καιροὶ ἐθνῶκ. καὶ πάλιν ›ὅταν δὲ ἴδητε κυκλουμένην ὑπὸ στρατοπέδων τὴν Ἰερουσαλήμ, τότε γνῶτε ὅτι ἤγγικεν ἡ ἐρήμωσις αὐτῆς‹. συγκρίνας δέ τις τὰς τοῦ σωτῆρος ἡμῶν λέξεις ταῖς λοιπαῖς τοῦ συγγραφέως ἱστορίαις ταῖς περὶ τοῦ παντὸς πολέμου, πῶς οὐκ ἂν ἀποθαυμάσειεν, θείαν ὡς ἀληθῶς καὶ ὑπερφυῶς παράδοξον τὴν πρόγνωσιν ὁμοῦ καὶ πρόρρησιν τοῦ σωτῆρος ἡμῶν ὁμολογήσας;

Eusebius is also interested in the account in the *Jewish War* of the celestial portents of doom to Jerusalem and its inhabitants (*B.J.* 6.288-304 in *H.E.* 3.8.1-9 [214, 26-220, 2]). He cites Josephus' narrative of the comet which hung over the city, the cow which gave birth to a lamb in the Temple, the phantasms and the mysterious voices which forboded the destruction of the city and the Temple. In the *Demonstration of the Gospel* 7.2 and the *Prophetic Excerpts* 3.46, Eusebius connects the destruction of Jerusalem with the destruction of the city and the sanctuary of Dan. 9:26. The bishop loosely cites *B.J.* 6.299 in which the priests at the daily sacrifice hear mysterious voices in the Temple speak, "We are departing hence."[49] (*D.E.* 8.2.121 [389, 31-35]; *Ecl. proph.* 3.46 [PG 22.1189]; *Chron.* [Jerome] 175.11-18). For Eusebius, even the heavens proclaimed the divine judgment descending over Jerusalem and the Temple.

In the *Ecclesiastical History,* Eusebius is even more interested in Josephus' account of the discovery of an oracle which predicted that a ruler would arise from Judea to rule the world (*B.J.* 6.312-313). Eusebius describes both the account in the *Jewish War* and Josephus' opinion that this ruler was Vespasian who was proclaimed emperor while conducting the war in Judea (*H.E.* 3.8.10-11 [220, 3-13]). As impressed as Eusebius is with Josephus' account of the oracle, he is not convinced that Vespasian was its object:

> Yet he did not rule over all the world but only over that of the Romans, and it would be more justly referred to Christ, about whom it was said by the Father, "Ask of me and I shall give you the nations to be an inheritance and the ends of the earth a possession." [Ps. 2:8] And it was of his holy apostles at that very time that "the sound went out into all the earth and their words to the ends of the world." [Ps. 18:5] (*H.E.* 3.8.11 [220, 6-13][50]

Not only was the fall of Jerusalem and the Temple predicted by Christ but to Eusebius the events surrounding their destruction, as witnessed by Josephus himself, testified to the lordship of Christ.

Eusebius on Moses and the Law

Josephus' treatment of Moses and the Jewish Law in *Against Apion* is the subject of great attention in the *Preparation for the Gospel* (also found in the *H.E., D.E.* and *Chron.* of Jerome). Josephus' purpose in *Against Apion,* to demonstrate the virtue of Judaism in the face of pagan claims to the contrary, parallels that of the *P.E.* Eusebius' goal for the *Preparation for the Gospel* is to

---

[49] μεταβαίνομεν ἐντεῦθεν.

[50] ἀλλ' οὐχ ἁπάσης γε οὗτος ‹ἀλλ'› ἢ μόνης ἦρξεν τῆς ὑπὸ 'Ρωμαίους· δικαιότερον δ ἂν ἐπὶ τὸν Χριστὸν ἀναχθείη, πρὸς ὃν εἴρητο ὑπὸ τοῦ πατρὸς ‹αἴτησαι παρ' ἐμοῦ, καὶ δώσω σοι ἔθνη τὴν κληρονομίαν σου, καὶ τὴν κατάσχεσίν σου τὰ πέρατα τῆς γῆς›, οὗ δὴ κατ αὐτὸ δὴ ἐκεῖνο τοῦ καιροῦ ‹εἰς πᾶσαν τὴν γῆν ἐξῆλθεν ὁ φθόγγος› τῶν ἱερῶν ἀποστόλων ‹καὶ εἰς τὰ πέρατα τῆς οἰκουμένης τὰ ῥήματα αὐτων‹.

demonstrate the superiority of Christianity's antecedent, i.e. Judaism, over its pagan rivals.[51] His logic is as follows: The religious opinions of the Greeks do not go back to the beginning of time and therefore cannot claim the authority of antiquity. The Jews, however, combine both antiquity and virtue in their laws and customs. One cannot allow the virtue and harmony of Jewish law and life while rejecting Jewish rites and culture or, put another way, it is not reasonable to vilify the Jews for their way of life and religious observances while recognizing the virtue of their laws. It should be noted that Eusebius is not making a case for Judaism in the *P.E.* but for Christianity. As Christianity has succeeded Judaism in the divine plan for world redemption in Eusebius' world view, Christianity has inherited all the virtues of its mother religion. Therefore, an assumption of the *Preparation for the Gospel* is that, if Judaism can be seen as superior to the paganism of its day, Christianity is likewise preferable given its ascendency over Judaism. This particular tenet is worked out in the theological sequel to the *P.E.*, the *Demonstration of the Gospel.*

As in Josephus' *Against Apion,* Moses here is the key to demonstrating the excellence of Jewish law. Eusebius cites *C.A.* 2.163-167 (*P.E.* 8.8.1-4 [433, 16-434, 9]) which puts the question "who was the most successful lawmaker and who attained the most accurate belief concerning God"[52] in order to answer it: Moses. Moses owed his success to the one God from whom all things were derived. Rather than put confidence in an imperfect monarchy or oligarchy, Moses' created a theocracy whereby all laws have their source in the ineffable and immutable Creator of all things.

Eusebius continues citing *Against Apion* (2.168-171 in *P.E.* 8.8.5-9 [1, 434, 9-26]). The Greeks themselves are not ignorant of the content of Moses' legislation for Pythagoras, Anaxagoras, Plato and the Stoics arrived at similar views of God. However, the failure of Greek philosophy and the success of Moses is evident in that the philosophy of the Greeks is comprehended only by the few whereas Moses' legislation is for all. Further, the laws left nothing to chance but ordered relationships between people as it established piety toward God.

Moses' skill as a lawgiver was matched by his sagacity in combining moral principles with education in living out the precepts of the Law (*C.A.* 2.171-178 in *P.E.* 8.8.9-13 [434, 24-435, 25]). For Moses, ignorance of the Law was unacceptable and therefore the Law became the central element in education. This stands in contrast to the Greek neglect of legal education where ignorance is the rule.

---

[51] For a discussion of the origins, style and sources of the *P.E.*, see E. H. Gifford, ed. and trans., *Eusebii Pamphili Evangelicae Praeparationis Libri XV* (Oxford, 1903), 3.1:v-xxx.

[52] *P.E.* 8.8.1 (433, 16-17) citing *C.A.* 2.163: ˜Τίς δ᾽ ἦν ὁ μάλιστα κατορθώσας τοὺς νόμους καὶ τῆς δικαιοτάτης περὶ τοῦ θεοῦ πίστεως ἐπιτυχών . . .

The result of the Mosaic system clearly demonstrates its superiority. The harmony and piety which exist in the Jewish community point to the perfection of the system which Moses created (*C.A.* 2.179-189 in *P.E.* 8.8.14-23 [435, 25-437, 13]). Although the Jews have been criticized for a lack of inventiveness, the drive to create the new is derived from the imperfection of the contemporary. As Moses laid down a perfect code, the Jews seek only to maintain what is flawless and thus desire nothing novel.

Eusebius' portrait of Moses or, rather, that created by Josephus which he borrows, is one of a wise man who legislates rather than the biblical image of the prophet who receives the Law by means of divine revelation. The Law has became the object of study in the academy with the aim to live a life of virtue, a goal which the hellenist would understand and grant approbation, and which meant keeping the Law: "For us, on the other hand, the only practical wisdom, the only virtue, is not to refrain from doing or thinking anything not laid down in the laws from the beginning" (*C.A.* 2.183 in *P.E.* 8.8.17 [436, 16-18]).[53]

The fountainhead of the Mosaic code is the Creator of all things, the ineffable God who is worshipped by the "practice of virtue"[54] (*C.A.* 2.193-198 in *P.E.* 8.8.24-27 [437, 13-438, 2]). This one God is served at one Temple whose sacrifices are models of propriety, unlike those of the Greeks, and prayers are offered for the good of the community, for the Jews are socially aware (*C.A.* 2.193-198 in *P.E.* 8.8.28-32 [438, 2-18]).[55]

Temple and cultus are followed by marriage laws (*C.A.* 2.199-203 in *P.E.* 8.8.32-36 [438, 18-439, 15]). Eusebius cites Josephus' narration that sexual relations serve only for procreation and sodomy stands as a capital offense. Courtship is described as is the submission of women to their husbands. Eusebius includes Josephus' confusing discussion of how birth and death require purifying ablutions for on both occasions a soul is leaving the body. In the former, the soul of the child leaves the womb of the mother and, in the latter, the soul is severed from the body by death.

The preceding discussion leads to the rearing of children. *C.A.* 2.204, cited in *P.E.* 8.8.37 (439, 15-20), notes that the birth of children is an occasion for sobriety and their education consists of training in the Law and the history of

---

[53] ἡμεῖς δὲ τοὐναντίον μίαν εἶναι καὶ φρόνησιν καὶ ἀρετὴν ὑπειλήφαμεν, τὸ μηδὲν ὅλως ὑπεναντίον μήτε πρᾶξαι μήτε διανοηθῆναι τοῖς ἐξ ἀρχῆς νομοθετηθεῖσιν.

[54] θεραπεύειν αὐτὸν ἀσκοῦντας ἀρετήν.

[55] H. St. J. Thackeray (*Josephus. The Life. Against Apion*, LCL [Cambridge, Mass. and London, 1926]) thought the final words of *C.A.* 2.198, ἃ μακρὸν ἂν εἴη γράφειν. τοιοῦτος μὲν ὁ περὶ θεοῦ καὶ τῆς ἐκείνου θεραπείας λόγος ἡμῖν ἐστίν, ὁ δ αὐτὸς ἅμα καὶ νόμος, were possibly an interpolation, owing to their absence from the major Eusebian mss. Given the occasional imprecision of Eusebius' citations, it seems more likely that Eusbius did not cite all of *C.A.* 2.198 and later redactors of the Eusebian text included the entire text from *Against Apion*.

their people. Josephus could have merely said that Jewish Scripture formed the basis of children's education but part of his argument for Jewish cultural superiority is that Jews are more knowledgeable of their laws than the Greeks and therefore observe them more closely.

As birth, the first major event for the soul, led to a discussion of child rearing, the severing of the soul from the body at death leads to a discussion of Jewish funeral customs (*C.A.* 2.205 in *P.E.* 8.8.38 [439, 20-440, 3]). Jewish funerals are characterized by their modesty. They are carried out by the relatives of the deceased but the community is involved. Finally the home and the immediate relatives of the deceased must be purified.

Honor due to one's parents and other social relationships are the subjects of *C.A.* 2.206-208 and *P.E.* 8.8.39-42 (440, 3-12). Next to God, the parents are to be honored by the son lest he be stoned. The young generally are to respect elders and friends are not to keep secrets from each other. For a judge to accept bribes is a capital offence. Theft, which includes usury, is singled out as a reprehensible crime.

The preceding passages from *Against Apion* cited in the *Preparation for the Gospel* serve less to explain Jewish law to Gentile readers than to convince them that Judaism is a philosophy characterized by harmony, reason and moderation, which leads to a life of virtue. Eusebius continues citing Josephus (*C.A.* 2.209-214 in *P.E.* 8.8.43-48 [440, 12-441,11]) to show that, although foreigners are not admitted into the Jews' most intimate affairs, the Law enjoins proper behavior extended additionally to others outside their religious family.[56] The Law requires that the Jews share the necessities of life with those in need and even enemies are accorded compassionate treatment. Jews must provide refuge to those who seek it and even beasts of labor are treated with kindness. The mercy of the Law is enforced and, as knowledge of the Mosaic code is part and parcel of the educational system, there can be no excuse for ignorance.

Eusebius cites Josephus' description of the severity of Jewish law (*C.A.* 2.215-217 in *P.E.* 8.8.48-49 [441, 11-18]): death is the usual penalty for transgressing, or intending to transgress, the most serious aspects of the Law. Even slaves are not exempt and the punishments for crimes such as fraud and theft are much more severe than in other legal systems. However, for those who observe the Law and who even die as a witness to it, God has promised a reward in a better life after death (*C.A.* 2.217-219 in *P.E.* 8.8.50-51 [441, 18-442, 5]).

As stated above, the point of Josephus', and therefore Eusebius', discussion of the Law was not to make the Mosaic legislation comprehensible but to affirm that one could not vilify what contributed to a life of virtue (ἀρετή). The

---

[56] If the exclusion of foreigners from the more intimate aspects of Jewish life was intended by Josephus to imply the exclusion of Gentiles from the Passover, one wonders what this passage meant to Eusebius. Like the Jews, Christians excluded pagans from their sacramental rites.

adumbration of the Law in *Against Apion* and the *Preparation for the Gospel* points to qualities of harmonious relations in the Jewish community, simplicity of lifestyle, discipline and sobriety. Eusebius continues citing from *Against Apion* where Josephus addresses the differences between the Greek and Jewish legal systems and the Greeks' dim view of the Jewish law (*C.A.* 2.220-228 in *P.E.* 8.8.51-55 [442, 5-443, 9]): the first difference between the two systems is that the Jewish system suggests an ideal government which would be considered fanciful except that it is known actually to exist. Jewish laws are far more stringent than Greek ones. Plato, for example, is much admired as a legal philosopher and yet his laws are more lenient than those of the Jews. Further, Plato hesitated to tell the masses about God in contrast to the Jews who make their theocratic system incumbent equally upon all. The second difference between the Greek and Jewish legal systems lies in the Jews' faithful adherence over the centuries to the Mosaic code in contrast to the Greeks' less faithful adherence to their code. Although the Spartans and Lacedaemonians are praised for their virtuous adherence to their laws, none have been more virtuous than the Jews for as long despite the numerous disasters which befell the Jewish people.

Scripture and Historical Writing

If Jewish virtue is based in part on the nature of the Law and the Jews' faithfulness in its observance, Eusebius, using *Against Apion,* also considers the antiquity of the Jews and the care exercised to preserve the record of their history (*C.A.* 1.6-14 in *P.E.* 10.7.1-10 [578, 9-579, 20]). Greek historical method is marred by the relative modernity of their culture, laws and historiographic accomplishments. Calamities have occurred which induced forgetfulness of the past such that each successive civilization has assumed it was the first. Compounded with this is the lateness of their acquisition of the alphabet which delayed historical writing. Homer is recognized as the earliest Greek poet and yet even he did not commit his works to writing. Numerous errors therefore crept into his epics. Greek historians wrote much later than the events which were the objects of their studies and the most ancient of Greek writings are thus subject to scepticism.

Further, the Greeks can make no claim to any special knowledge of antiquity for their historians cannot come to a consensus on any historical account (*C.A.* 1.15-16 in *P.E.* 10.7.11-14 [579, 20-580, 15]). *H.E.* 3.10.1-5 (222, 22-224, 15), citing *C.A.* 1.38-42, points out that, since the Jews have only twenty-two books of sacred origin which are in harmony and have been transmitted carefully over the years by the Jewish community, this has resulted in greater diligence in maintaining their accuracy. The Greeks, on the other hand, have many historical works which reflect mere personal opinion and therefore less care has been observed in their transmission. Discrepancies among Greek historians can be explained in part by the absence of public records (*C.A.* 1.19-21 in *P.E.* 10.7.15-17 [580, 15-581, 3]). Even the Athenians were not given to maintain an account of their history and the Arcadians were so late in learning to write that their claim to antiquity is not worthy of mention (*C.A.* 1.22 in *P.E.* 10.7.18 [581, 3-4].

If Greeks came to keep records many years after the events recounted by the historians, Greek historical writing also suffered from too great a concern for style at the expense of accuracy (*C.A.* 1.23-26 in *P.E.* 10.7.19-21 [581, 5-17]). Josephus and thus Eusebius grant that the Greeks are the most able and eloquent of writers but leave much to be desired in terms of reliability.

Biblical Chronology and Geography

If Eusebius uses Josephus to denigrate the alleged superiority of Greek historians and historiography, the bishop also finds him useful with regard to the reliability of Scripture. Josephan material serves two functions: (1) Josephus, as a recognized historian, can confirm the accuracy of biblical assertions. Interestingly, it does not strike Eusebius as absurd to use Josephus to confirm the accuracy of the Bible, upon which Josephan literature is itself dependent. (2) The Jewish historian provides supplementary material on chronological and geographical matters not found in Scripture.

With respect to chronological matters, Eusebius mentions in the *Chronicle* that Josephus dated the construction of the first Temple 240 years after the founding of Tyre (*A.J.* 8.62; *Chron.* [Jerome] 55a.22). Further, considerable similarity exists between *A.J.* 11.111-112 and *H.E.* 1.6.5-6 (50, 5-11) which loosely traces Judean government back from Herod to Moses.

Eusebius employs the *Antiquities* in his *Onomasticon*. Mt. Ararat in Armenia and its significance in the Noah pericope (Gen 8:4) is explained. Josephus' account, described as being found in the first book of his *Antiquities*, is interwoven in Eusebius' narrative (*A.J.* 1.92; *Onom.* 4.2-25). The identification of biblical Arkem as Petrea is attributed to Josephus (*A.J.* 4.82; *Onom.* 36.13-14 on 2 Kgs 17:30). *A.J.* 8.163 narrates the sending of ships by Solomon to the land of Sopheir in India. *Onom.* 150.14-18 (on Gen 10:30) notes this account and summarizes it (*Onom.* 160.19-20 on 1 Kngs 9:28 also notes Sopheir's location as India without mentioning Josephus). Josephus' description of the Tigris (*A.J.* 1.39) is mentioned in *Onom.* 164.8-9 (on Gen 2:14). *Onom.* 60.3-4 identifies the Egyptian river Gaion as the Greek Nile. Given its certain use for the Tigris, it seems possible that *Antiquities* 1.39 is the source here as well. The same case can be made for Eusebius' identification of the Phison as the Ganges (*A.J.* 1.38; *Onom.* 166.7 on Gen 2:11).[57]

---

[57] H. Schreckenberg (*Die Flavius-Josephus-Tradition in Antike und Mittelalter* [Leipzig, 1972], 80-81), following Klostermann in the GCS, has identified a number of other passages from the *Onomasticon* which parallel the *Antiquities*. There is nothing to recommend inclusion with those passages considered above except that Josephus was evidently a frequently used source for the *Onomasticon*.

Josephus and Biblical Narratives

Eusebius also makes use of a series of biblical episodes narrated in the *Antiquities*. Josephus' function is to confirm the accuracy of the biblical accounts. That Josephus himself employed Jewish Scripture and thus is not an independent witness to the Bible's accuracy is not an issue for Eusebius. Josephus also serves as an intermediary source for other witnesses to events recounted in Scripture.

Eusebius cites two passages from the *Antiquities* on Noah and the flood: *A.J.* 1.93-95 in *P.E.* 9.11.1-4 (497, 13-26) and 1.105-108 in *P.E.* 9.13.2-5 (499, 6-19). In the first, Josephus is himself citing other witnesses to the flood. Josephus quotes Berosus the Chaldean and Nicolaus of Damascus while mentioning Hieronymus of Egypt and Mnaseas. The second is Josephus' own information regarding the considerable longevity of the antedeluvian generations asserted by the Bible and his claim that support for this phenomenon can be found in the writings of Manetho, Berossus, Molos, Hestiaeus, Hieronymus the Egyptian, Hesiod, Hecataeus, Hellanicus, Acusilaus, Ephorus and Nicolaus of Damascus.

Josephus narrates the account of the Tower of Babel and its location in *A.J.* 1.117-119. The entry in the *Onomasticon* for Babel (Βαβέλ; Gen 11:9) cites *A.J.* 1:117-118 (*Onom.* 40.11-19) which identifies the place of the Tower of Babel as that which became Babylon. Further, Eusebius' discussion of Shinar (Σενναάρ; Gen 11:2ff.) cites *A.J.* 1.119 to the effect that the plain named Senaar was in the region called Babylon (*Onom.* 148.13-17). The *Preparation for the Gospel*, concerned with finding extrabiblical support for the biblical account of the Tower supposedly written by Moses, notes Josephus' identification of the word "Babel" (Βαβέλ) with "Babylon" (Βαβυλών) in *A.J.* 1.117.

The *Demonstration of the Gospel* and the *Onomasticon* show interest in Josephus' account in *Antiquities* 1.122-150 of the nations which are descended from Noah's sons. *D.E.* 4.3.6 (410, 4) informs the reader of Josephus' explanation of the Iberians' descent from Thobel (θοβέλ; θεόβηλος in *A.J.* 1.124). *Onom.* 82.2-3 considers that the name of the land Εὐειλάτ[58] (Gen 2:11) is derived from one of Noah's sons and notes that Josephus related that the sons of Noah inhabited the regions from the Euphrates to the Indian Ocean (*A.J.*

Ultimately, however, it cannot be determined whether or not they have their source in the *Antiquities*.

A.J.	9.245	*Onom.*	6, 18	Gen 14:1.	Location of Eilat
	9.7		86, 18	Jos 15:62	Description of Engedi
	2.257		124, 8	Gen 25:2	Location of Madiam
	1.336		150, 24ff.	Gen 14:6	Location of Seir
	4.82-83		176, 7	Nu 20:22, 28	Death of Aaron occurred near Petra.

[58] MT: חֲוִילָה

1.143).[59] *Onom.* 150.14-17 notes the same passage from *Antiquities* considering the location of Sephar (Σωφειρά; Gen10:30) as does *Onom.* 176.15-16 which deals with origin of the name Opheir ('Ωφείρ; 1 Kngs 9:28).

Onomasticon 100.23ff. is concerned with the location of Tarshish (1 Kngs 10:22). Eusebius notes Josephus' comment that Ταρσός, also known as θάρσος, is another name for Cilicia (*A.J.* 1.127).

Ur of the Chaldees (Οὒρ τῶν Χαλδαίων; Gen 11:28) is the subject of *Onom.* 140.12-14. It is identified as the place where Arran, the brother of Abraham, died as reported by Josephus (*A.J.* 1.151).

Moses is not the only biblical figure of interest to Eusebius. The *Preparation for the Gospel* cites *A.J.* 1.158-161 which contains testimony by Berosus and Nicolaus of Damascus on Abraham (*P.E.* 9.16.2-5 [501, 6-21]). Berosus notes Abraham's Chaldean origins and his astrological expertise. Nicolaus describes Abraham as an invader from the Chaldees who settled with his family in Canaan, called Judea. The Damascene also mentions that Abraham is well known in Damascus where a village is named "Abraham's dwelling" ('Αβράμου οἴκησις λεγομένη).

Eusebius cites Josephus' account in *Antiquities* of Abraham's success in Egypt and how he instructed the Egyptians in mathematics and astronomy, originally Chaldean sciences, after resolving undisclosed customs practiced by contending Egyptian parties (*A.J.* 1.165-168 in *P.E.* 9.16.6-8 [502, 1-11]). These sciences were then passed on to the Greeks. Thus not only do the Greeks owe a debt to the Jews for their philosophy but even their knowledge of the sciences originated with the father of the Jewish people.

Another biblical theme figures in the *Demonstration of the Gospel. D.E.* 6.18.36-37 (281, 5-13), citing *A.J.* 9.224-225, deals with the story of King Uzziah who offered sacrifice in the Temple and was punished with leprosy (2 Chr 26:18-20). Josephus' account in *Antiquities* differs from the biblical one only in that he expands several details. *Antiquities* maintains that Uzziah threatens the priests with death unless they cease their interference with his sacrifice; concurrent with Uzziah's attempt to usurp the priestly prerogatives is an earthquake (cf. Zech 14:5). Zech 14 prophesies a war waged against Jerusalem by the Gentiles which, along with a concomitant earthquake like that in the days of King Uzziah, would herald the coming reign of God and the exaltation of Israel. If Josephus is not interested in the oracle, the author of the *Demonstration of the Gospel* certainly is. Although Eusebius does not indicate why he prefers the Josephan account to the biblical one, his interest in the destruction of Jerusalem and its link with Jesus may provide an answer. Eusebius could have drawn a connection between the Josephan account, which mentions Zech 14 and, to Eusebius assuredly messianic, prediction of war and

---

[59] *Selection from Histories* in Cramer, 2:170 paraphrases *A.J.* 1.143ff.

divine deliverance, and the Roman siege of Jerusalem for it was Jesus, the holy one of God, who predicted the destruction of the city. To the objection that the nature of God's deliverance in Zech 14 is fundamentally different from the Christian understanding of deliverance through Christ, Eusebius would probably respond that this points out the obscure character of biblical prophecy. Unknowingly, Josephus has made a connection which serves one of the purposes of the *Demonstration of the Gospel:* to show that Old Testament prophecy has been fulfilled in Jesus.

In a discussion of the rebuilding of the Temple, the *Demonstration of the Gospel* notes that Josephus details the completion of the Temple during the reign of Darius (*D.E.* 8.2.65 [379, 11ff.]). More interesting, however, is Eusebius' remark that Josephus narrated how Alexander the Great arrived in Jerusalem and worshipped God (*D.E.* 8.2.67 [379, 28-380, 1]). The Josephan account not only has Alexander worship but sacrifice as well (*A.J.* 11.336). What is important is that both Eusebius and Josephus share the same apologetic needs.

Material from Other Ancient Witnesses

It has already been noted that the *Preparation for the Gospel* is essentially an anthology of ancient opinion which serves to make Eusebius' point that the Jews constitute a virtuous people of greater antiquity than the Greeks; and their laws are not merely older but more harmonious and contributory to a life of virtue than the legislation of the Greeks. Not only does Eusebius utilize Scripture and Jewish authors such as Philo and Josephus but also opinions of "objective" non-Jewish historians of note to support his claim of Jewish antiquity. However important a work the *Preparation for the Gospel* may be for having transmitted excerpts of literature, some otherwise unknown, it is hardly the first of its type. Indeed, *Against Apion* also musters historical testimony from the ancients to illustrate the same point that Eusebius seeks to demonstrate: the superiority of Jewish life and law flows from its virtue and its antiquity which go back to Moses from whom even luminaries such as Plato drew knowledge. Not only does *Against Apion* provide Eusebius with a model for demonstrating the antiquity and virtue of the Jews, but Josephus offers material from other historians as well. Like *Against Apion,* the *Preparation for the Gospel* offers testimony from Greek, Chaldean, Egyptian and Phoenician historians. Eusebius uses Josephan material albeit in an order of his own fashion.

Eusebius cites Hecataeus of Abdera who wrote regarding the dimensions of Jerusalem and the Temple along with the story of Mosollamus the archer who served in the army of Alexander the Great (*C.A.* 1.197-204 in *P.E.* 9.4.2-9 [490, 1-491, 12]). The passage from Hecataeus points to the magnificence of the Jewish capital and the Temple as well as the shrewdness of the Jewish archer who demonstrated the absurdity of looking to nature for signs and portents.

Clearchus, a peripatetic and student of Aristotle, wrote a book entitled *On Sleep* (Περὶ ὕπου) in which a statement regarding the origins of the Jews is attributed to Aristotle (*C.A.* 1.176-179 in *P.E.* 9.5.1-12 [491, 13-492, 5]). The Jews are said to be descended from Indian philosophers which points to great antiquity and a long philosophical tradition. Thus we find a philosophical notable attesting to Josephus' and Eusebius' claim.

Eusebius cites a passage from the poet Choerilus who, when writing of Xerxes' expedition against Greece, mentions that among his troops were those who lived "in the Solymian hills by a broad lake"[60] (*P.E.* 9.9.1-2 [494, 19-495, 10]). The bishop's comments on the passage bear considerable verbal similarity to Josephus' own remarks which identify the Solymian hills as Jerusalem and the broad lake as the Dead Sea (*C.A.* 1.172-174).

Eusebius concludes his treatment of Greek witnesses to Jewish antiquity by citing the conclusion to his consideration of the similar section in *Against Apion* (*C.A.* 1.215-218 in *P.E.* 9.42.1-3 [553, 11-554, 6]). Eusebius, drawing from what he calls the *Archaeology of the Jews*, lists Greek authors not included in his text who misrepresented the facts but nevertheless attested to the Jews' antiquity.

We have already noted Eusebius' use of Berosus the Chaldean who dated Abraham to the tenth generation after the flood (*A.J.* 1.158 in *P.E.* 9.16.2 [501, 6-9]). Berosus' account of Nebuchadnezzar's capture of various nations, including the Jews, is cited as Josephan without further attribution to Berosus (*C.A.* 1.136-137 in *P.E.* 9.40.1-2 [549, 4-11]).[61] Eusebius seems to have missed Josephus' note that he was citing Berosus (*C.A.* 1.133). Eusebius again cites from *Against Apion* without noting that the material originates with Berosus (*C.A.* 1.146-153 in *P.E.* 9.40.3-11 [549, 13-550, 22]). This passage traces Babylonian rule from the death of Nebuchadnezzar to Cyrus during whose reign the Temple was rebuilt. The only sign in the *Preparation for the Gospel* that Eusebius is aware of Josephus' transmission of Chaldean material is a note that Josephus appends to his treatment of Phoenician historians testimonies for the antiquity of the Jews from the histories of the Chaldeans (*P.E.* 10.13.13 [609, 5-7]; cf. *C.A.* 1.128).

Josephan material drawn from Berosus is also used in the Armenian *Chronicle* (21.1-23.29; 24.29-25.5; cf. *C.A.* 1.128-134). Unlike the *P.E.*, attribution is made here to Berosus and this material on the life of Nebuchadnezzar is included in a rather longer account than is to be found in *Against Apion*. Eusebius' fascination with Nebuchadnezzar comes from his role in Daniel (*Chron.* [arm.] 20.24ff.). Berosus' material thus serves as a gloss on the biblical account.

---

[60] ἐν Σολύμοις ὄρεσι πλατέη παρὰ λίμνῃ.
[61] It is evident that Eusebius utilized *C.A.* rather than its parallel in *A.J.* 10.221-222 given the numerous differences between the two Josephan texts.

Eusebius also cites portions of Josephus' narrative drawn from Manetho the Egyptian (*C.A.* 1.73-75, 82-90, 103-105 in *P.E.* 10.13.1-12 [606, 18-608, 25]). The antiquity, hence authority, of Manetho is beyond all doubt and his discussion of the Hycsos is of interest regarding the identification of the Hebrews. Manetho noted that the Hycsos were a shepherd people who were expelled from Egypt after wresting the government of the land from native Egyptians. Josephus' analysis of Manetho's material (which is what attracts Eusebius' attention), identifies the Hycsos as the Hebrews.

The Armenian *Chronicle* also makes use of the material in *Against Apion* from Manetho (*C.A.* 1.73-105; *Chron.* [arm.] 70.3-74.6). Unlike the *Preparation for the Gospel,* which is interested only in establishing the identification of the Hycsos as the Hebrews, the *Chronicle* includes more of the narrative account of Egyptian history, given its less narrowly defined chronographic interests.

Josephus' material in *Against Apion* drawn from Phoenician writers also makes an appearance in the *Preparation for the Gospel* and the Armenian *Chronicle. P.E.* 10.13.13 (609, 2-5), presents Tyrian evidence that the Temple of Solomon was constructed 143 years and 8 months after the founding of Carthage (*C.A.* 1.108 or126). The Armenian *Chronicle* (25.6-24) makes reference to an unidentified Phoenician document in *C.A.* 1.155-160[62] which establishes that 54 years separated the destruction of the Temple and the reign of Cyrus. The Temple is also the subject of *Chron.* (arm) 54.1-56.19 which cites *C.A.* 1.106-127.[63] Josephus cites Tyrian evidence for relations between King Hiram and Solomon at the time of the Temple's construction. Testimony of the Phoenician historians Dius and Menander of Ephesus is cited as additional evidence. Josephus seeks to demonstrate the antiquity of the Jewish nation, for Hiram's accession to the throne occurred 155 years and 8 months before the founding of Carthage (*C.A.* 1.126). Further, the construction of the Temple took place only after the Jews consolidated their hold of the land which was many years after their entry into it (*C.A.* 1.127). To Eusebius, this fits in with the purpose of the *Chronicle* which is to place the story of the Jews in the context of general history and to offer incontrovertible evidence of their antiquity.

Conclusion

We have seen that Josephan material provided Eusebius with considerable data. We find background material which expands upon biblical accounts, historical narrative on persons and events in Jewish history contemporaneous with Jesus as well as geographical and chronological information. However,

---

[62] H. St. J. Thackeray suggests in his translation of *Against Apion* that the passage is from Menander of Ephesus (p. 225, note e).
[63] Also found in the *Selection from Histories,* Cramer, 2:184-187.

Josephus' more significant contributions to Eusebius derive primarily from the former's account of the siege of Jerusalem in the *Jewish War* and the defense of Jewish antiquity in *Against Apion*. With regard to the siege of Jerusalem, Eusebius' concern is to illustrate fulfillment of Jesus' prophecy regarding the destruction of the Jewish capital (Mark 13, Matt 24 and Luke 21) which would be a sign of the approach of the Kingdom. The *Ecclesiastical History* is Eusebius' account of the unfolding of that fulfillment. Josephus stands as an eyewitness to what Jesus had prophesied and the tragedy which overtook the Jewish people. Unlike Josephus who was concerned to depict the horror of the siege, Eusebius' focus is on the unfolding of the Kingdom of which the destruction of the city is but a sign. Eusebius must also explain why the catastrophe occurred. Origen had declared that the murder of James the Just was the cause of the city's destruction. However righteous a man James had been, it must have seemed remarkable to Eusebius that his death should bring on such a catastrophe (after all, the deaths of Peter and Paul did not cause the destruction of Rome). Further, the prophecy regarding the destruction of Jerusalem is part of larger discussion of the coming time between Jesus' departure (i.e., his death) and his return to earth in power and glory. It would have been reasonable for Eusebius to relate the catastrophe which befell Jerusalem to the death of Jesus. Indeed, the Gospels are eager to point out Jewish responsibility for the death of Jesus (cf. Matt 27:24-25). What is remarkable is not that the destruction of Jerusalem was seen by Eusebius as punishment for the crucifixion of Jesus but that the theme was not developed earlier. To illustrate the enormity of this crime, the bishop includes the earliest known citation of the *Testimonium Flavianum* to provide objective and reliable testimony by this noted Jewish historian to the true nature of Jesus.

The second major Josephan contribution to Eusebius lies in the latter's use of *Against Apion* to establish Jewish, and therefore Christian antiquity. The *Preparation for the Gospel*, the first part of Eusebius' grand scheme to demonstrate the antiquity and virtue of Christianity over its pagan rivals, utilizes Josephus' own argument as well as testimony from earlier authors whom Eusebius cites through *Against Apion*. Josephus' apology for the greater antiquity of Moses and the superiority of the Jewish law and customs over those of the Greeks finds its way directly into Eusebius' argument. Further, ancient witnesses to Jewish antiquity, not all complimentary, are laid out by Josephus and borrowed by Eusebius. Josephus' apology for Judaism becomes Eusebius' apology for Christianity as the child has inherited the antiquity and the virtue of the parent whom it has replaced in God's plan for the redemption of the world.

What is remarkable is that this is a significantly different role for Josephus than we have seen before. We no longer see Josephus cited merely as a famous and highly regarded Jewish historian; rather Eusebius has fully appropriated him for the Church. Josephus described the world depicted in the Gospels and was witness that Jesus was the Christ. Further, he described the destruction of

Jerusalem which was construed as punishment for the murder of Jesus by the Jews. Finally, he wrote an apology for his religion which has been absorbed into the defense of Christianity against paganism. Eusebius, more than anyone else, brought Josephus into the Church where he would be preserved and studied.

Part Two

SUMMARY

Chapter Fourteen

Josephus as a Source

The fundamental question in assessing Josephus' impact on early Christian literature is to determine the extent to which we can be certain that the authors under consideration actually read Josephus. Indeed, it is impossible to evaluate the literature examined to this point without clearly ascertaining which material is relevant to our subject.

Our Christian authors fall into one of five possible categories: (1) Given the paucity of evidence, the writer probably did not use Josephan material. The evidence may even suggest a source common to both our Christian and Josephus. (2) The writer is acquainted with Josephus but does not reveal any genuine knowledge of Josephan material. (3) The author probably did not read Josephus but unknowingly used material from a secondary source drawn from the Josephan corpus. (4) The writer probably made use of Josephus. (5) The writer clearly made use of material drawn from Josephus. A writer who falls into the first category is of no significance given our purposes. A Christian author in the second category is a witness to Josephus' stature among historians in late antiquity. With respect to the third possibility, that the writer unwittingly used Josephan material, what interests us is the identity of the intermediary source. Of greatest interest are those writers who fit into the fourth and fifth categories since their use of Josephus was intentional.

A further complication in assessing the influence of Josephus on Christian literature concerns the poor state of that literature's preservation. As we have seen, some works exist only in fragments or in translation. Naturally, we cannot speculate as to what no longer exists but the limited amount of textual evidence combined with its poor quality can make the determination of whether or not Josephus was indeed a source little more than speculative. We shall, nevertheless, identify each of the Christian authors with an eye to distinguishing which offer clues for our understanding of Josephus' impact on Christian literature through Eusebius.

(1) *The writer probably did not use Josephan material given the paucity of evidence.* The fourth-century rhetorician, Lactantius, understands the "sons of God" of Gen 6:2 to be angels who, after being enticed by the devil, cohabitated with women against the wishes of God. Given the absence of verbal similarity

with Josephus' own interpretation of the biblical passage, the differences in detail between *A.J.* 1.73 and *Divine Institutes* 2.15 and the identification of the "sons of God" with angels elsewhere in the literature of late antiquity, it would be folly to assume dependence upon Josephus. Hippolytus also may belong in this category. His account of the Essenes in the *Philosophoumena* may share a common source with that of the *Jewish War* or may depend upon a source which made use of material in *B.J.* Nevertheless, there is no evidence that he was directly acquainted with Josephus' account of the Essenes.

(2) *The writer is acquainted with Josephus but does not reveal any genuine knowledge of Josephan material.* The second-century bishop of Lyons, Irenaeus, knows that Josephus wrote of Moses' campaign in Egypt. Given Irenaeus' penchant for using a doxography, we cannot say how well acquainted he really was with Josephus. Minucius Felix also betrays no knowledge of Josephus except that he was a historian of the Jewish War who was respected by the Romans. Pseudo-Justin is aware that Josephus wrote of Moses in his *Antiquities* but does not rely on the Josephan account for any material.

(3) *The author probably did not read Josephus but unknowingly used material drawn from the Josephan corpus.* Hippolytus may have used a source for information about the Essenes which contained material from the *Jewish War*. This is more likely than assuming both he and Josephus used a common source given that this otherwise unknown source would have had to survive another 150 years after Josephus.

(4) *The writer probably made use of Josephus.* The second-century Melito of Sardis appears to have made use of Josephus' account of the siege of Jerusalem in the *Jewish War*. In *On the Passion*, Melito refers to the privations suffered during the siege culminating in occurrences of cannibalism. The story of a mother caught devouring her child figures prominently. Melito does not cite any text other than Scripture and although the destruction of Jerusalem was recounted elsewhere in Christian, Jewish and pagan sources, the details of his account of the siege seem to have been most likely drawn from *B.J.* 6. Nevertheless, Melito may not have made direct use of the *Jewish War* and therefore should be placed in the preceding category.

(5) *The writer clearly made use of material drawn from Josephus.* The second-century bishop of Antioch, Theophilus, was considerably influenced by *Against Apion*. In the third book of *To Autolycus* he closely follows the argument of *C.A.* to demonstrate the antiquity of the Jews although he freely summarizes the text. Theophilus utilizes *C.A.* 1.93-102 where Josephus cites the Egyptian Manetho. Although Manetho is not complimentary to the Jews, he is an important witness to Jewish antiquity for both Josephus and Theophilus. He follows *Against Apion* in summarizing Tyrian evidence for the antiquity of the first Temple (*To Autolycus* 3.22; *C.A.* 1.106-126). Theophilus departs somewhat from *Against Apion* in providing a biblical chronology from Adam to the Babylonian exile (3.24-25) while Josephus refers his readers to the

Antiquities (*C.A.* 1.127). The Antiochene summarizes the major points of Josephus' history regarding the exile, the rise of Persia and the rebuilding of the Temple (3.25; *C.A.* 1.128-154). Finally, the Chaldean Berosus is cited in support of the biblical accounts of the Flood, the Babylonian exile and the Persian period (3.29; *C.A.* 1.128ff). Despite Theophilus' free rendering of material from *C.A.* and discrepancies between *To Autolycus* and *Against Apion* (many of which appear to be scribal in origin), the Antiochene occupies a significant place in our study for he was the first among extant Christian authors to adopt *Against Apion* as a model for Christian apologetics. We shall not see another Christian borrow so much of Josephus' apology until Eusebius in the fourth century. In this respect Theophilus was very much ahead of his time.

In the *Miscellanies*, Clement of Alexandria poses an interesting problem: he states that Josephus calculated the period from Moses to David to be 585 years. Since no such calculation is to be found, one might suppose that Clement has either misread Josephus or his text is different from any we now possess. As we have seen, Clement derived his calculations from *B.J.* 6 and *A.J.* 8 although his arithmetic is in need of correction.

Another Alexandrian, Julius Africanus, made use of Josephan material from *A.J.* 12 on the period from Alexander to Herod. Other fragments of the *Chronography* do not demonstrate dependence on Josephus but, given the paucity of the evidence, we cannot know to what extent Julius may have employed Josephus.

The most infamous of the Alexandrians, Origen, poses difficulties in that we can be certain that Josephus was the source for certain material but not for other data. We find that *Against Apion*, the *Jewish War* and the *Antiquities* were employed by Origen in *Against Celsus* and in his commentaries on Lamentations, Song of Songs, Matthew and John. It is possible that Origen used some Josephan material secondhand. If he did use a doxographical work or cite Josephus through some lost work, it is nevertheless clear that he was well acquainted with the ultimate source of the material. Nevertheless, at times we cannot be certain if Origen is thinking of a Josephan source: *Comm. Jn.* 6.9 deals with the revolts of Theudas and Judas the Galilean. Although one is tempted to suggest dependence on *A.J.* 20.97-102, there is nothing which indicates that Origen used any material beyond Acts 5. Further, *Comm. Jn.* 13.39 notes that Passover occurs during the month of Nisan. Although *A.J.* 3.248 and 249 indicate this, there is no reason to suppose Origen's knowledge of the Jewish calendar or religious practices must be derived from Josephus despite the prominent position of the Jewish historian in Origen's writing. Origen's sources are not always identified and we must not fall into the trap of assuming Josephan dependence without attribution or verbal similarity.

A noteworthy aspect of Origen's use of Josephus is his willingness to impose a meaning on the Josephan text based upon an interpretation of its significance. Origen understands the destruction of Jerusalem by the Romans as punishment for the death of James the Just and attributes this opinion to Josephus (*C. Cels.* 2.13). The Alexandrian also attributes to Josephus an identification of the murdered Zechariah (Matt 23:35) as the father of John the Baptist (Katenen fragment 457.2). As we have seen, Josephus does discuss the murder of Zecharias, son of Baris (*B.J.* 4.335-344). Origen notes the similarity of names and makes the identification on that basis. Origen also alters Josephus' account of the affair of the standards (*B.J.* 2.169ff. and *A.J.* 18.55ff.), having the effigies of the emperor brought into the Temple and not merely into Jerusalem (*Comm. Mt.* 17.25). The Josephan narrative may not be dramatic enough for Origen or perhaps, as the Temple figures prominently in Jesus' predictions of the destruction of Jerusalem, Origen is drawing a connection between the Temple and the events which eventually would lead to its destruction. The possibility exists that Origen's misstatements of what Josephus actually wrote were derived from an intermediate source. However, we cannot say who that intermediate source might have been; moreover citations we find in Origen's works from Josephus demonstrate essential agreement with existing Josephan texts. It seems reasonable that Origen himself was responsible for these attributions which, interestingly, all relate to the New Testament. Josephus is being employed as support for Origen's understanding of particular aspects of New Testament history or prophecy (the destruction of Jerusalem). We shall observe this same technique in Eusebius, the best known of Origen's followers.

Methodius clearly cites *B.J.* 6.435-437 in *On the Resurrection* 3.9.15-21 to refute Origen who had interpreted the dry bones pericope in Ezekiel 37 as pertaining to the return from the Babylonian exile rather than, as more commonly understood by this time, the resurrection from the dead. The passage from the *War* indicates that Jerusalem was destroyed subsequent to the return from the Babylonian captivity and, to Methodius' mind, this indicates that the promise of Ezekiel 37 was not fulfilled upon the return from Babylon. As we have already indicated, Methodius' use of Josephus may reflect the latter's importance for Origen. Origen drew a connection between the siege of Jerusalem in the *Jewish War* and the desolation of Jerusalem in Lamentations (*Comm. Lam.*). Methodius may be attempting to refute Origen with material favored by the latter.

Eusebius represents the culmination of what trends we have already noted. We shall discover how certain themes evolving in early Christian literature achieved their characteristic form with Eusebius. It should be stated that Eusebius' genius was synthetic rather than creative in nature. Theologically he was an Origenist and his task as a historian was to synthesize various traditions into a picture of orthodoxy which endures in the Church. Eusebius' use of Josephus was to incorporate throroughly the Jewish historian into his account of the *Heilsgeschichte* of the Church. As already noted, Eusebius was generally faithful to the Josephan text. It remains a possibility that Eusebius may have come by some of his Josephan material secondhand; however, we are incapable of confirming this. Both the limited amount of manuscript evidence and the non-extant Greek originals of the Eusebian corpus (particularly the *Chronicle* which exists in the Latin version by Jerome and in the Armenian) ultimately leave this question unanswerable. Nevertheless, the extensive number of citations and the extent to which Eusebius makes use of Josephan material suggests that Eusebius was thoroughly familiar with Josephus' works.

We shall consider how Eusebius made use of Josephan material as we detail the development of those themes in Christian literature to which Josephus made a contribution. However, we shall first examine the differences between the use of Josephan material in the literature of the Christian East and his impact on the literature of the Christian West.

Chapter Fifteen

Josephus in the Literature of the Christian West

A startling difference between our western and eastern authors lies in the minimal use of Josephan material by the former as compared to the latter. In the West, only Irenaeus, Minucius Felix and Tertullian clearly knew anything of Josephus; Hippolytus' account of the Essenes remains of dubious value. There is no compelling evidence to suggest that Hippolytus was acquainted with Josephus' account of the Essenes. If he and Josephus shared a common source, Hippolytus may have been totally unfamiliar with Josephus' narrative. Likewise, if Hippolytus used a source which itself drew from the Josephan account, we can discern no sign that he was aware of the ultimate source as he seeks to portray Judaism as a collection of fragmented sects. We must also exclude Lactantius from consideration in that there is no evidence that he derived any information from Josephus.

The second-century Irenaeus refers to Josephus' account of Moses' Egyptian campaign where Moses was aided by an Ethiopian princess whom he subsequently married. Irenaeus' information is part of what appears to be an exegetical piece on Numbers. Given this most meagre reference, the absence of a citation and Irenaeus' penchant for utilizing doxographical materials, it would be unwarranted to hazard a guess that the *Antiquities* was the source of Irenaeus' knowledge.

Minucius Felix also can tell us but little. The third-century apology *Octavius* addresses the contention that the superiority of the Roman deities over the God of the Jews (and Christians) is demonstrated by Jerusalem's destruction at the hands of the Romans. The author finds Josephus useful only in that he can be summoned as an expert on the siege of Jerusalem who can attest to the wickedness of the Jews who got their just desserts (*Oct.* 33). Minucius attributes the destruction of the city to their abandonment of God. The *Octavius* does not cite from Josephus any particular evils perpetrated by Jerusalem's defenders which would be *a propos* his point. One is generally inclined to question whether Minucius had read Josephus' narrative or was simply aware of it secondhand.

Tertullian demonstrates more awareness of Josephan material than does Minucius Felix. Like the author of the *Octavius*, Tertullian offers an apology of

Christianity to silence its pagan critics. However, unlike Minucius Felix, he does not use Josephus to point out the wickedness of Jews but, rather, introduces the "vindicator" of his people who, by extension, will also vindicate Christianity (*Apol.* 19). Tertullian notes that Moses can be traced back to King Inachus and antedated the Argive king Danaus by almost 400 years (according to *C.A.* 1.103 and 2.16, the period was 393 years). Tertullian is apparently aware that Josephus either confirmed or refuted the testimonies of Manetho the Egyptian, Berosus the Chaldean, King Hiram of Tyre, Ptolemy of Mendes, Demetrius Phalereus, King Juba, Apion and Thallus. Tertullian constructs his list by summarizing the ancient writers treated by Josephus in *C.A.* 1 and 2. Tertullian does not follow the Josephan order and mistakes Thales for Thallus (*C.A.* 1.14). Further, as noted in the analysis of the *Apology* 19, Josephus does not consider Ptolemy of Mendes in *Against Apion* nor does he discuss Juba (although he is to be found in *B.J.* 2.115 and *A.J.* 17.349). Through Tatian (*Ad Graec.* 38) we know that Ptolemy deemed Moses to be a contemporary of the Argive king Inachus. Juba was, according to Pliny, a prolific historian. Perhaps he wrote of the Jews and thus was, along with Ptolemy of Mendes, included in Tertullian's list for that reason.

Tertullian is the sole example of a Christian writer in the West before Eusebius who clearly made use of more than Josephus' name and reputation. His limited use of *Against Apion* indicates that he had accepted Josephus' apology as a model useful for the Church against the pagan charge that Christianity was not old enough to claim any authority. The assumption in the hellenistic mind that antiquity conferred authority had already been addressed by Josephus who argued in *Against Apion* for the antiquity of Moses and the Mosaic code. Josephus sought to establish the greater antiquity, and hence greater authority, of Judaism over Hellenism. Tertullian concluded that if Josephus' argument is valid for Judaism, it was also applicable to Christianity. Of interest is that the link between Judaism and Christianity is assumed rather than explicitly demonstrated. Tertullian, unlike Minucius Felix who had to deal with the theological implications of the destruction of Jerusalem and the Temple, had no interest in distancing Christianity from Judaism. The theological concept of the Church as the "new Israel" was taken for granted as Josephus was enlisted to defend Christianity.

If the evidence from the Christian West indicates that Josephus had no observable impact there beyond Tertullian, this stands in contrast to the East to which we now turn.

Chapter Sixteen

Josephus in the Literature of the Christian East

Josephus influenced the Christian literature we have examined in three not unrelated areas: (1) apologetics, (2) biblical exegesis and chronography, and (3) accounts of the destruction of Jerusalem. With regard to apologetics, Josephus' primary contribution was *a propos* the question of Christianity's authority to confront hellenistic philosophy and religion whose obvious claim to antiquity conveyed authority. In order to refute the charge of the hellenists that Christianity was far too novel to be taken seriously, it was necessary for Christian apologists to respond as did their Jewish counterparts. Christianity had to be not only as ancient as its pagan rivals, but even older. The obvious fact that Christianity could not trace its history beyond the first century C.E. did not deter the Christian apologists. The Christian self-understanding of the Church as the "new Israel" served to establish continuity with the religion of the Jews. Indeed, what is noteworthy is not that this concept was held (Rom 11:17 describes the Gentiles as the wild olive branch grafted onto the tree which is Israel and in Gal 6:16, Paul addresses the Church as the "Israel of God")[1] but that the apologetic literature does not explain and defend what would have seemed a historical fiction to any pagan reader. It is reasonable that the Hellenists might not have clearly distinguished between Christianity and Judaism in the first century C.E.; however, this hardly seems plausible from the mid-second century on. The only reasonable conclusion is that the apologetic literature we have examined was intended less for a pagan audience than for a Christian one. The only attempt in the literature we have examined to separate Judaism from Christianity was that of Minucius Felix who had to explain how the destruction of the Second Temple was not a defeat of the God of the Old and New Testaments (the Jews were so thoroughly wicked that God abandoned them to their fate). Except for the *Octavius,* it was accepted *a priori* that Christianity was the heir to God's promise to Abraham. Given this, what is surprising is not that *Against Apion* should be accepted as a model for apologetic literature but that it should have taken as long for this to occur as it did.

---

[1] τὸν Ἰσραὴλ τοῦ θεοῦ.

Until Origen, Josephus' influence on Christian exegesis was minimal. We shall find some concern for chronographical issues; however, in that chronography places biblical and intertestamental history in the context of world history (thus confirming biblical antiquity), it is akin to apologetics. Chronography served the need of Christians to have an understanding of their history and antiquity. However, chronography is not merely a variant of apologetics. Chronography also reflects the Christian movement toward a soteriological understanding of God's redemption of humankind unfolding through Israel and through the Church.

Third, the theme of the destruction of Jerusalem emerges as more than merely the fulfillment of a prophecy made by Jesus. For the evangelists, the destruction of the city and Temple could not be seen as a defeat of their god by Rome and, therefore, was presented as part of God's purpose and even as having been predicted by the Christ. This explanation, however, was inadequate to later generations of Christians who discerned other implications in the event. The ongoing interpretation of the event is an indication of Judaism's place in the evolving Christian *Heilsgeschichte.* Josephus' account of the siege and destruction of Jerusalem became inextricably bound up with the Christian interpretation of the tragedy.

Josephus and the Christian Apologist

We have established that Pseudo-Justin's *Exhortation to the Greeks* was a fourth-century work incorrectly ascribed to the second-century Justin Martyr. The *Exhortation* evinces possible dependence upon Julius Africanus and may be the lost work *On Truth* (Περὶ Ἀληθείας) by the Syrian Apollinarius which responded to the Emperor Julian's edict of 362 C.E detailed in Sozomen's *Ecclesiastical History* 5. The ascription to Apollinarius is no more than plausible; nevertheless, it raises the possibility that the *Exhortation* does not fall in within our time frame. Therefore, we must be careful not to accord too much weight to the evidence of Pseudo-Justin.

The purpose of the *Exhortation* was to demonstrate the bankruptcy of Hellenistic thought by revealing internal contradictions in Greek philosophy and the ridiculous image of the deities in Greek poetry. That many hellenists would have agreed with Pseudo-Justin regarding the portrayal of their gods and that Christianity was not as internally consistent as Pseudo-Justin would have the readers believe, does not deter him. Pseudo-Justin is heir to the hellenistic tradition of the sage dating back to Hecataeus of Abdera who portrays Moses as a wise man and philosopher. Pseudo-Justin's Moses antedates the Greek philososphers; accordingly, the superior authority of Christianity, the "true" Israel, is confirmed (Moses is described as "our" first prophet). Josephus is named as a recognized historian who had narrated the life of Moses. There is no evidence that Pseudo-Justin had any real knowledge that Josephus developed the theme of the greater antiquity, and hence greater authority, of Moses in *Against*

Apion. Pseudo-Justin's argument could very well have been drawn from a common Christian trope and his awareness of Josephus might be secondhand (possibly from Julius Africanus who certainly made use of Josephus).

As already noted, the second-century bishop Theophilus of Antioch was the first Christian writer clearly to make extensive use of *Against Apion.* Josephus is a major source in Theophilus' *To Autolycus* which attempted to demonstrate the greater antiquity and concomitant primacy of Christianity over paganism. Theophilus introduces Josephus as having authored an account of the Jewish War; however, as we have seen, more important to Theophilus is Josephus' dating of the biblical books as antecedent to the Trojan War in *Against Apion.* Theophilus also includes material from *Against Apion* originating with Manetho as well as a summary of Tyrian evidence on the antiquity of the Temple. There is nothing startling in the argument of *To Autolycus;* noteworthy is the extent to which Theophilus obviously made use of *Against Apion* in the second century C.E.

The major difficulty in assessing the influence of Josephus upon Clement of Alexandria lies in the extremely wide range of material used by Clement in his *Miscellanies* and the extent to which he paraphrased them without making attribution. Josephus appears in the *Miscellanies* in connection with Clement's chronographic endeavors. Clement seeks to parallel biblical events with events in world history whose dates are established. Josephus provides the numbers necessary for Clement to calculate the time span from Moses to Vespasian. Although the *Miscellanies* shares characteristics with the apologetic literature we have seen (i.e., Moses is depicted as antedating the Greek philosophers), Clement appears to be genuinely interested in the dates of biblical history. He demonstrates a more sophisticated approach to historical writing and a more refined apologetic which goes beyond the immediate apologetic needs of a new religion to withstand attack by an older and established paganism. Clement shows signs of interest in a Christian self-definition which would culminate in the theological understanding of history we discover in Eusebius.

The evidence of Julius Africanus is frustrating on account of its limitations. The African makes considerable use of *A.J.* 12 on the period from Alexander to Herod; however, in that the *Chronology* is extant only through citations in other writers we cannot ascertain to what extent Julius may have made use of Josephan material. As already stated, Clement presented a picture of a Mosaic system whose origins stretch back into antiquity and the African carried out Clement's schema in great detail. That Julius' interests, like those of Clement's, go beyond merely defending Christian antiquity is indicated by the details from Josephus' narrative on the Tobiads that we find in the fragments from the *Chronology.*

The third Alexandrian, Origen, adds little to what we have already seen with regard to apologetics. *Against Celsus* requires evidence for the antiquity of Moses, which Origen finds in *Against Apion.* Origen must defend the antiquity of Judaism and places the Jewish people among the acknowledged ancient

Egyptians and Phoenicians. Moses is presented as a wise man, a figure well-known in the hellenistic world. *Against Apion* is also utilized to demonstrate that the biblical account of the Flood, Mosaic in origin, is more accurate than that of the Greeks. Of interest here is the increasing use of *Against Apion* as source-book and model for Christian apologetics. More creative, however, is Origen's use of Josephan material to confirm the biblical narrative. We now turn to this.

Josephus and the Christian Exegete

Origen makes use of the *Jewish War* and the *Antiquities* in his biblical commentaries. In his commentary on Matthew, Origen ascribes the destruction of Jerusalem to the death of James the Just and attributes the interpretation of the event to Josephus (see following section on the theme of Jerusalem). Origen narrates the Josephan account of the standards (*B.J.* 2.169ff. and *A.J.* 18.55ff.) but has the Roman standards brought not merely into the city of Jerusalem but into the Temple area.

The Alexandrian also indulges in creative exegesis. Origen identifies the innocent Zechariah, son of Berachiah, of Matt 23:35 with Zecharias, son of Baris, whose murder by the Zealots is recorded in *B.J.* 4.335-344. In his commentary on Song of Songs (*Cant. Cantic.* 2), Origen recounts the visit to Solomon of the Queen of Sheba. The Alexandrian identifies the biblical Sheba with the Ethiopian city of Saba (*A.J.* 8.165ff.). Origen's motivation in finding extrabiblical confirmation in Josephus for these biblical accounts is not simply apologetic in nature but, rather, is that of the historian seeking to expand upon the biblical witness.

Origen used the account of Jerusalem's siege (*B.J.* 6.201-213) in his commentary on Lamentations (*Comm. Lam.* 105). The Alexandrian compares the pitiable state of Jerusalem during the Babylonian siege to that during the siege by the Romans. The commotion before the altar which heralded the divine abandonment of the sanctuary in *B.J.* 6.299 appears in *Comm. Lam.* 109, and *Comm. Lam.* 115 notes how "Josephus recorded the story of those who fled into the hills" (possibly relating to *B.J.* 5.446ff.). As we have noted, Origen is seeking to add historical detail to the biblical witness. To do so with the Babylonian siege of Jerusalem is difficult except that the Josephan account of the Roman siege of the city can provide detail which seems applicable to the earlier siege. There is even a similar theological perspective on the cause of the two disasters. Origen considers pride and violence of the wicked to be behind the disaster which overtook the city (homily on Ps 73) while Josephus narrated the heinous crimes of Jerusalem's defenders in the *Jewish War*.

Josephus and the Siege of Jerusalem

The interpretation of the siege and destruction of Jerusalem comes to be a measure of the status of Judaism in Christian theology. However, this was not an early development. Jesus' prediction of the destruction of Jerusalem and the Temple which we find in the Gospels served to address the issue of what Jerusalem's destruction meant to a Church not yet totally separated from the mother-faith in the latter decades of the first century C.E. To the evangelists, what must have been seen as a tragedy by Jewish-Christians was transformed into part of God's plan of redemption foreseen by the Christ himself. In the preceding chapter, we noted that the Roman jurist Minucius Felix went beyond the evangelists and addressed the implication that the destruction of the Temple signified a defeat of the God of the Jews and the Christians. The *Octavius* makes it clear that the destruction of the city and Temple occurred because the Jews had abandoned God and, as a result, were themselves abandoned. Minucius Felix was, however, less concerned with understanding the status of Judaism in Christian thought than with dealing with the notion, which he accepted without reservation, that the destruction of a nation implies a defeat of that nation's deity or deities.

Melito's *On the Passion* echoes the Josephan account of Jerusalem's sins which preceded the city's destruction. If Melito did make use of the *Jewish War,* his purpose was to paint a portrait of a people damned by sin and whose deliverance could be effected only by the Christ. Melito's narrative is not concerned with the Jews but with corrupt humanity which is in need of the Christ-event, a Passover to deliver humankind from sin and death.

Origen departs from an understanding of the destruction of Jerusalem which has its roots in the New Testament. For the Alexandrian, the conspiracy of the high priest and others which resulted in the death of James the Just was the cause for the city's destruction. *Against Celsus* 2.13 goes so far as to state that it was Josephus himself who offered this interpretation. Our discussion of Origen's use of Josephan material indicated that Origen felt free to take liberties in adapting Josephus to his purposes. Given this, it seems likely that Origen himself was responsible for this opinion rather than some lost version of the *Antiquities* which differed considerably from the extant texts.

Methodius' citation of *B.J.* 6.435-437 (in *On the Resurrection* 3.9.15-21), which summarizes the number of times that Jerusalem was captured before being taken in the second year of Vespasian's reign, may speak to the importance of Josephan material for Origen. It is but an appendix to Origen's use of the historian.

Just as with apologetics and exegesis, we must now turn to Eusebius in order to see how the theme of the destruction of Jerusalem developed and what impact Josephus had on it.

Chapter Seventeen

Josephus and Eusebius

As we have previously stated, Eusebius' contribution to Christian literature was his synthesis of intellectual currents existing in the Church. A caution, however, is appropriate at this point. We must not assume that Eusebius was incapable of creativity. If Eusebius' mind was of a synthetic bent, it must be remembered that history as a discipline is essentially synthetic in nature. We shall consider several concepts in Eusebius' use of Josephan material we have not encountered before. The origin of these ideas, if it is not Eusebian, eludes us. Nevertheless, Eusebius offered a definition of orthodoxy which Christianity adopted and Eusebius is thus a significant milestone on the way from an evolving Christian consciousness to a normatively defined Christianity. It remains for us to examine the three areas of apologetics, exegesis and treatment of the destruction of Jerusalem to discern the impact of Josephus in the work of this pivotal figure.

Josephus and Eusebian Apologetics

Eusebius presents Moses as a wise man whose genius lay in skillful legislation. In this the Alexandrian departs from the biblical portrait of the lawgiver as the receiver of revelation and has placed Moses in the academy and made the Law an object of study whose aim is to promote a life of virtue (ἀρετή). We have seen the antiquity of Moses defended in order to legitimize Judaism and, by extension, Christianity; however, the *Preparation for the Gospel* goes beyond this in portraying the lawgiver as the ultimate philosopher. Pseudo-Justin does present Moses as a wise man but does not develop the theme to any length comparable to that of Eusebius. Clement offers the closest parallel to the Eusebian testimony although his portrayal of Moses as the philosopher to whom the Greeks are indebted is also not as extensive as that of Eusebius. It is this element that marks Eusebius' work as truly significant. Eusebius' depiction of Moses is not novel as the image of Moses as a philosopher was a standard trope of hellenistic-Jewish apologetics. However, the bishop's use of this theme is novel given its importance in his argument. Although Eusebius' work is synthetic in nature, particularly the *Preparation for the Gospel,* this does not account entirely for the prominence of this theme. This is something we have not seen before in the extant Christian literature.

Moses, according to Eusebius, is the one who created a perfect legal system in that it works (as opposed to that of the Greeks). The Law is strict and applied equally to all, commends a life of morality and sobriety, requires that all study its precepts, and encourages harmony. All of these features contrast with the Greek laws which cannot match the accomplishments of the Mosaic code.

If the philosophical accomplishments of Moses and the harmonious perfection of the Law go beyond what we have seen to date in the Christian literature we have examined, they should be familiar to us from *Against Apion.* That the purpose of the Law is to promote virtue is drawn from *C.A.* 2.183. *Against Apion* 2 provides Eusebius with all the elements of his argument which appears in the *Preparation for the Gospel.* In earlier Christian literature we have seen *Against Apion* used to defend the antiquity of Judaism. Eusebius goes beyond this and utilizes *C.A.* to defend Judaism's character.

Abraham, Josephus' subject in *A.J.* 1, becomes the figure which Eusebius uses to defend Jewish antiquity. *P.E.* 9.16.6-8 cites Josephan material which describes how Abraham taught the Egyptians the Chaldean sciences of mathematics and astronomy which were later transmitted to the Greeks. Not only are the Jews more ancient but the Greeks owe a debt to the Jews for their scientific knowledge. This is more in keeping with what we have seen heretofore, especially with regard to Clement, although it is Eusebius who has introduced Abraham into the discussion.

Eusebius also introduces another element drawn from *Against Apion* into his apology in the *P.E.* and that is the historical accuracy of biblical literature as opposed to the literature of the Greeks. We have seen a similar theme in Pseudo-Justin who contrasted the harmony among Jewish writers with the contradictions in Greek poetry and histories.

With regard to apologetics, we have seen that Eusebius has borrowed a significant portion of his argument in the *Preparation for the Gospel* from *Against Apion.* In that the *P.E.* is an anthology, one can say of course that the entire argument is borrowed from someone. However, Eusebius has introduced a thoroughly hellenized portrait of Moses as preeminent philosopher into Christian literature and the portrait was that of Josephus. Eusebius went beyond the corollary that antiquity confers authority to depict as well the character of the legislation. In that the Mosaic code is more likely to engender virtue in the adherents of the Law, it is both superior to as well as older than Greek law and philosophy. This is Josephus' argument in *Against Apion* and, through Eusebius, it has become an argument of Christian apologetics. Although Paul does find that the Jewish Law serves a positive function, Eusebius' assertion is noteworthy given Christian diatribes against the Law.

As mentioned above, Eusebius' portrayal of Moses as wise man parallels that of Pseudo-Justin's in his *Exhortation to the Greeks.* In our discussion of the *Exhortation,* we considered the difficulty of establishing a date for this work. Nevertheless, we assigned Pseudo-Justin to approximately the same period as

Eusebius. Whether we are seeing a relationship between the *Preparation for the Gospel* and the *Exhortation* (i.e., one read the other or they are both borrowing from *C.A.*) is impossible to determine. We can say, however, that in Eusebius we encounter the earliest *developed* expression of this trope in extant Christian literature.

Josephus and Eusebian Exegesis

Eusebius devoted considerable attention to exegesis and Josephus played a far greater role in his writings than what we have seen heretofore. In our discussion of Eusebius we saw that in the *P.E.* and the *D.E.* the bishop made use of a series of episodes from the *Antiquities* which confirm biblical narratives. Noah and the Flood, the nations which descended from Noah's sons, Abraham in Egypt, King Uzziah and the building of the Second Temple make their appearance. Eusebius' gives away part of his purpose in his discussion of King Uzziah (*D.E.* 6.18.36-37): to demonstrate that Old Testament prophecy was fulfilled in Jesus. We might be tempted to accept this as the chief element in Eusebius' idea of history (Christian theology has long treated the Old Testament as a book of prophecies relating to Jesus). However, Eusebius' use of the Jewish Scripture and Josephus' confirmation of biblical narratives goes beyond this narrow focus. Eusebius is interested in historical detail because he understands history to be the area where God works out His purposes. Therefore, Eusebius sees Scripture as a record of *Heilsgeschichte* whose accuracy Josephus can supplement and confirm.

Eusebius also finds Josephus useful with respect to the events narrated in the New Testament (specifically the Gospels). We have seen chronicled, particularly in the *Ecclesiastical History* but also in the *Demonstration of the Gospel* and the *Chronicle,* events antedating the birth of Jesus. Josephus provided Eusebius with material on the Hasmoneans, Herod the Great's origins and reign as well as the disposition of his kingdom after his death. Eusebius' interest in Herod is understandable given the king's role in Jesus' birth narratives in the Gospels. Further, Josephus provides material on the census, Annas and Caiaphus (material which Eusebius uses to clarify the reading of Luke 3:2) and John the Baptist.

In selectively using Josephus for historical background, Eusebius is able to ignore conflicts between Josephus and the New Testament. In the case of John the Baptist, Eusebius simply does not note the differences between the Gospels and *Antiquities* on the matter of Herod Antipas' marriage to Herodias. Further, Eusebius can use Josephan material on Pilate as a gloss on the Gospels so as to endorse the Josephan portrait of Pilate as a reprehensible figure despite the more positive portrayal of the procurator in the Gospels. Gamaliel's speech in Acts 5:34-39, commenting on the revolts of Theudas and Judas the Galilean, incorrectly reverses their sequence. Eusebius' response to the contradiction between Acts and *Antiquities* is to cite Josephus' account of Theudas' rebellion

(*A.J.* 20.97-98) while ignoring Josephus' information on Judas. It is not surprising that Eusebius would gloss over these differences although his apparent agreement with Josephus' estimate of Pilate against that of the Gospels is worthy of comment. The relatively positive portrayal of Pilate in the Gospels, as opposed to those of Josephus, Philo (*Legatio* 38) and Tacitus (*Ann.* 15), was certainly influenced by the evangelists' attempt not to antagonize Rome by accusing the procurator of killing Jesus. The situation was certainly different by Eusebius' time and the bishop was certainly freer to offer a more objective portrayal of Pilate.

If Eusebius felt free to gloss over differences between the New Testament and Josephus, he also offers evidence of having tampered with the Josephan material or of possessing a version of Josephus somewhat different from that which we now possess. Josephus' account of Agrippa's death in *A.J.* 19.343-351 is at odds with the story of Acts 12. In *Antiquities* it is an owl which is the harbinger of Agrippa's death while an angel occupies the role in Acts. Eusebius cites but modifies the Josephan text so as to bring Josephus into conformity with Acts (*H.E.* 2.10.1-9). As was the case with Origen, Eusebius cites the affair of the standards (*B.J.* 2.156-170) and has them brought not merely into Jerusalem but into the Temple area (*H.E.* 2.6.4). Given Eusebius' inclination for Origenistic theology, it seems quite likely that he was familiar with Origen's variation on the Josephan narrative (*Comm. Mt.* 17.25). Eusebius also includes an unknown citation attributed to Josephus which describes James the brother of Jesus as "the Just" (*H.E.* 2.23.20). As previously noted in the analysis of this passage, we may be dealing with a body of tradition surrounding James and the destruction of Jerusalem which is reflected in Origen, Hegesippus and Eusebius. Nevertheless, we cannot discount the possiblity that Eusebius himself was the source of this spurious Josephan citation.

The *Testimonium Flavianum* remains the most significant and the most problematic of passages, for several reasons: (1) It is present in all the extant manuscripts of the *Antiquities* and (2) it seems incredible that Josephus could have written it. Although in this study we have assumed that Josephus could not have been the author of the passage, successful ascription remains elusive.[1] One is left to wonder if this spurious citation found its way into the manuscript tradition owing to some derogatory remarks original to *A.J.* 20.

Eusebius, like the Alexandrians Clement and Julius Africanus, is interested in chronography although Josephus occupies a rather limited role therein. As with the recounting of episodes in biblical history, Josephus is appropriated to confirm the accuracy of Scripture. The bishop is unconcerned that Josephus

---

[1] For a bibliography of the problem and study of why the *Testimonium Flavianum* should not be attributed to Josephus, see Paul Winter, "Excursus II--Josephus on Jesus and James *Ant.* xviii, 3, 3 (63-4) and xx 9, 1 (200-3)," in E. Schürer's *The History of the Jewish People in the Age of Jesus Christ,* G. Vermes, F. Millar and M. Black, eds. (Edinburgh, 1973), 1:428-441.

himself utilizes the biblical narrative and, as such, is hardly an objective witness. *Against Apion* 1 is helpful in establishing the date of the building of the First Temple (*P.E.* 10.7.15-17). This gives Eusebius an opportunity to note the antiquity and accuracy of Jewish records (as opposed to those of the Greeks).

Even more important to the bishop than chronography is biblical geography; the *Antiquities* makes a contribution to those sections of the *Onomasticon* dealing with Genesis. Eusebius seems to be relying on Josephus' authority as a historian of antiquity. Eusebius' preoccupation with both biblical geography and chronography attest to his interest in the *Heilsgechichte* portrayed in Scripture and Josephus' role in confirming its accuracy and supplementing its detail.

Josephus and Eusebius on Jerusalem

Of the Christian writers we have encounted in this study, Eusebius is the first to devote attention to the events which preceded and precipitated the Jewish War. Eusebius cites Josephus' account of the violence among the priests at Jerusalem (*H.E.* 2.20.1-3; *A.J.* 20.180-181) and the activities of the Sicarii (*H.E.* 2.20.4-6; *B.J.* 2.254-256). The reason for their inclusion is probably that they occurred during the procuratorship of Felix who is treated in Acts. Josephus' account of the false Egyptian prophet also makes an appearance in the *Ecclesiastical History* (*B.J.* 2.261-263; *H.E.* 2.21.1-2). This prophet is present in Acts 21:38. One might suppose that Eusebius' interest in these matters was occasioned by his interest in the Acts of the Apostles.[2] However, *H.E.* 2.26 deals with the procurator Florus (*B.J.* 2.284, 306-308) and the death of the Syrian Jews (*B.J.* 2.461-465). The bishop is presenting his readers with the unfolding fulfillment of prophecy.

Eusebius depicts the siege of Jerusalem as the fulfillment of Jesus' prophecies in the Gospels. Like the Gospel account, the bishop notes that the catastrophe had been brought about due to the sinfulness of the populace; however, the people's crime is bringing about the death of Jesus (*H.E.* 3.7.1). Eusebius is not unaware of the earlier interpretation of the event by his mentor Origen and Hegesippus which attributed the catastrophe to the death of James the Just, for the bishop cites Hegesippus' comment that upon James' death the armies of Vespasian besieged Jerusalem (*H.E.* 2.23.18). The issue for Hegesippus is that the punishment should follow immediately upon the crime and not a generation later. To Eusebius, Josephus' stories of the comet which hung over the city, the cow giving birth to a lamb and especially the mysterious voices heard in the Temple which proclaimed "We are departing hence" (all from

---

[2] One is inclined to wonder if this passage from the *Jewish War*, which the bishop may connect with Acts 21, not only influenced the Eusebian account but the text of Acts as well. See notes 21 and 31 in the chapter on Eusebius.

B.J. 6) confirm the imminence of an act of divine judgment (*D.E.* 8.2.121; *Ecl. proph.* 3.46; *Chron.* [Jerome] 175.11-18).

Matthew 24:19-21 was not the only prophecy fulfilled in the destruction of Jerusalem. The *Preparation for the Gospel* 7.2 and the *Prophetic Excerpts* 3.46 connect the destruction of Jerusalem and the Temple by the Romans with the destruction of the city and Temple in Daniel 9:26. For Eusebius, the gruesome details of destruction, suffering, cannibalism and the statistics of the dead and those enslaved in the aftermath in *H.E.* 3 (all drawn from the *Jewish War*) fit the apocalyptic vision of Daniel. Eusebius juxtaposes Daniel's promise of deliverance with the prophesy of a world ruler (whom Josephus identified with Vespasian [*B.J.* 6.312-313]) and identifies the figure as the Christ. Given that the magnitude of the disaster of 70 C.E. prompted attention to the prophecy in Daniel, and given that Jesus was alleged to have predicted the event in great detail, for Eusebius the destruction of Jerusalem emerges as a testimony to the lordship of Christ which is itself confirmed by the oracle predicting the rise of a world ruler out of Judea.

Josephus and the Eusebian Legacy

We have examined Josephus' impact on Eusebius but a final assessment requires that we recapitulate what we have already discovered. Before Eusebius, Josephus was enlisted primarily to demonstrate that Christianity, as the heir of Judaism, could claim the requisite antiquity to be authoritative. Except for a few cases where Josephus provided historical background, not much was done with Josephus beyond this apologetic function outside the Alexandrian School. The Alexandrians show more interest in Josephus as a source for historical background to the biblical narrative as well as interest in chronographic matters. Nevertheless, Josephus was most useful in establishing Jewish, and therefore Christian, antiquity. Eusebius was responsible for expanding the use of Josephan material and, as Eusebian literature came into broad use, so did that of Josephus.

Eusebius followed in established tradition and used *Against Apion* as evidence for Jewish antiquity and its concomitant authority; however, he also employs Josephus' apology for Judaism in a new way by arguing for the moral superiority of Judaism. This is not to suggest that Christian apologists had not advocated Christianity's morality in the face of immoral paganism or that Christian writers had portrayed Judaism as morally inferior to Christianity. There is nothing novel in Eusebius' assertion that Hellenism had received what truth it possessed from the arch-philosopher Moses, although it is noteworthy that Eusebius draws his entire argument in the *Preparation for the Gospel* from *Against Apion*. However, Eusebius does make it clear that the Church had inherited more than Judaism's antiquity: it also received from the preparatory Jewish religion a moral tradition superior to that of Hellenism.

Relating to exegesis and biblical history, Eusebius also expanded the use of Josephus as a source for background material. We did not find any use of Josephus in earlier writers comparable with that in Eusebian literature.[3] Further, Eusebius' interest in Jewish history preceding the birth of Jesus and his elaboration of New Testament and early Christian history is in itself noteworthy and his employment of Josephan material commended the Jewish historian to later generations of Christian exegetes and historians.

Finally, Eusebius' treatment of the siege and destruction of Jerusalem is a less felicitous epilogue to this study. Certainly the destruction of the city and the Temple was an event of considerable theological significance for Christianity. The Gospels seem to address the question by having Jesus predict it, thereby mourning what had been brought about by the Jews' sinfulness, and construing it as a part of the unfolding *Heilsgeschichte*.[4] This, however, was certainly insufficient for later generations of Christians who sought a more profound interpretation of the event. Origen and Hegesippus understood it to be an act of divine retribution for the death of James the Just. Eusebius, on the other hand, saw the event in the apocalyptic terms of Daniel. The destruction of Jerusalem was too significant an event not to be connected with the Christ who had predicted and mourned its coming. Further, the Josephan tradition of prophecy which heralded the rise of a world ruler from Judea was connected with the Christ. Eusebius, or whoever may have authored the concept, made the people's transgression to be the crucifixion of Jesus. Josephus, as Eusebius' source for details of the tragedy, was thus made to serve the anti-Jewish sentiment within the Church.

---

[3] It has been noted that Hegesippus wrote a now lost work on the Jewish sects (*H.E.* 4.8) which means that Eusebius was not the first Christian author interested in this period. However, we know nothing of its nature.

[4] Regarding Matt 22:2-24, which indicates that the destruction of Jerusalem was an act of divine retribution, see note 2 in "Introduction and Methodology."

Bibliography

Altaner, B. *Patrologie.* 2nd ed. Freiburg: Herder, 1950.

_____. *Patrology.* 5th English ed. Trans. H. C. Graef. Freiburg: Herder, 1960.

Asmus, J. R. "Ist die pseudojustinische Cohortatio ad Graecos eine Streitschrift gegen Julian?" *ZWT* 38 (1895):115-155.

_____. "Eine Encyklika Julians des Abtrünnigen und ihre Vorläufler." *ZKG* 16 (1895-96): 45-71 and 220-252.

_____. "Ein Bindeglied zwischen des pseudojustinischen Cohortatio ad Graecos und Julians Polemik gegen die Galiläer." *ZWT* 40 (1897): 268-284.

Axelson, B. *Das Prioritätsproblem Tertullian-Minucius Felix.* Lund: H. Ohlssons, 1941.

Baehrens, W. A., ed. *Origenes Werke. Achter Band. Homolien zu Samuel I, zum Hohelied und zu den Propheten. Kommentar zum Hohelied in Rufinus und Hieronymus' Übersetzung.* GCS 33. Leipzig: J. C. Hinrichs, 1925.

Bardenhewer, O. *Geschichte der altchristlichen Literatur.* 2 Vols. Freiburg: Herder, 1902.

Bardy, G.. "Mélanges: Le souvenir de Josèphe chez les Pères." *RHE* 43 (1948): 179-191.

Baylis, H. J. *Minucius Felix and his Place among the Early Fathers of the Latin Church.* London: S.P.C.K., 1928.

Beaujeu, J. *Minucius Felix: Octavius.* Paris: Sociéte d'Edition "Les Belles Lettres," 1964.

Black, M. "The Account of the Essenes in Hippolytus and Josephus." In *The Background of the New Testament and its Eschatology,* ed. W. D. Davies and D. Daube, 172-175. Cambridge: Cambridge University Press, 1956.

Blank, J. *Meliton von Sardes Vom Passa, Die älteste christliche Osterpredigt.* Sophia 3. Freiburg im Breslau, 1963.

Bonner, C. *The Homily on the Passion by Melito of Sardis with Some Fragments of the Apocryphal Ezekiel.* Vol. 12 of Studies and Documents, K. Lake and S. Lake, eds. London: Christophers, and Philadelphia: University of Pennsylvania Press, 1940.

Bonwetsch, G. N. *Methodius.* GCS 27. Leipzig: J. C. Hinrichs, 1917.

Buchheit, V. *Studien zu Methodius von Olympos*. TU 69. Berlin: Akademie, 1958.

Burchard, C. "Die Essener bei Hippolyt, Ref. IX 18 2-28 2 und Josephus, Bell. 2,119-161." *JSJ* 8 (1977): 1-41.

Cadiou, R. *La Jeunesse d'Origène: Histoire de l'Ecole d'Alexandrie au début du IIIe Siècle*. Paris: G. Beauchesne, 1936.

Chadwick, Henry. *Early Christian Thought and the Classical Tradition. Studies in Justin, Clement, and Origen*. New York: Oxford University Press, 1966.

Clark, Elizabeth A. *Clement's Use of Aristotle: The Aristotelian Contribution to Clement of Alexandria's Refutation of Gnosticism*. New York: E. Mellen, 1977.

Cramer, J. A., ed. *Anecdota graeca e codd. manuscriptis bibliothecae regiae Parisiensis*. 4 Vols. Oxford, 1839-41.

Cruice, P. *Philosophoumena*. Paris, 1860.

Curtius, E. R. *Europäische Literatur und lateinisches Mittelalter*. 7th ed. Bern: Franke, 1969.

Diels, H. *DoxographiiGraeci*. Bern, 1948.

Dindorf, G., ed. *Georgias Syncellus et Nicephorus CP*. Vol. 21 of the Corpus Scriptorum Historiae Byzantinae, ed. B. G. Niebuhr. Bonn, 1829.

Dräseke, J. "Der Vefasser des fälschlich Justinus beigelegten ΛΟΓΟΣ ΠΑΡΑΙΝΕΤΙΚΟΣ ΠΡΟΣ ΕΛΛΗΝΑΣ." *ZKG* 7 (1884-85): 257-302.

Dunker, L. and F. Schneidewin, *S. Hippolyti . . . Refutationis Omnium Haeresium*. Göttingen, 1859.

Feldmann, L. *Josephus and Modern Research*. Berlin: W. de Gruyter, 1984.

Gager, J. G. *Moses in Greco-Roman Paganism*. Nashville: Abingdon, 1972.

Gaisford, T., ed. "Ecologae Propheticae." In *Eusebii Pamphili . . . Tomus Quartus*. PG 22:1017-1262. Paris, 1857.

Gelzer, H. *Sextus Julius Africanus und die Byzantinische Chronographie*. 3 Vols. Leipzig: J. C. Hinrichs, 1885-98. Reprint. New York: Burt Franklin, 1967.

Gifford, E. H., ed. and trans. *Eusebii Pamphili Evangelicae Praeparationis*. 4 Vols. Oxford, 1903.

Grant, Robert M. "Irenaeus and Hellenistic Culture." *HTR* 42 (1949): 48-51.

_____. "Notes on the Text of Theophilus, To Autolycus III." *VC* 12 (1958): 136-144.

_____. "The Textual Tradition of Theophilus of Antioch." *VC* 6 (1952): 146-159.

Gressman, H., ed. and trans. *Eusebius Werke. III. Band 2. Hälfte. Die Theophanie. Die Griechischen Brüchstücke und Übersetzung der Syrischen Überlieferungen.* GCS 11.2. Leipzig: J. C. Hinrichs, 1904.

Gutschmid, A. von. *Kleine Scriften.* Vol. 5. Leipzig, 1894.

Hall, S.G. "Melito in the light of the Passover Haggadah." *JTS* n.s. 22 (1971): 29-46.

_____. *Melito of Sardis. On Pascha and Fragments.* Oxford: Clarendon Press, 1979.

Harnack, A. *Die Chronologie der altchristlichen Literatur bis Eusebius.* Leipzig: J. C. Hinrichs, 1904.

_____. *Geschichte der altchristlichen Litteratur bis Eusebius.* 2 Vols. Leipzig: J. C. Hinrichs, 1893.

_____. *Die griechische Übersetzung des Apologet. Tert.'s.* TU 8:4. Leipzig: J. C. Hinrichs, 1892.

_____. "Die Überlieferung der griechischen Apologeten des 2. Jahrhunderts in der alten Kirche und im Mittelalter." TU 1:100-300. Leipzig: J. C. Hinrichs, 1883.

Hasi, C. B., ed. "Index Scriptorum." In *Leonis Diconi Historia . . .* PG 117:1215-1424. Paris, 1894.

Havercamp, S., ed. *Flavii Josephi Opera.* Amsterdam, 1726.

Heikel, I. A., ed. *Eusebius Werke. Sechster Band. Die Demonstratio Evangelica.* GCS 23. Leipzig: J. C. Hinrichs, 1913.

Heinze, R. *Tertullians Apologeticum.* Leipzig: B. G. Teubner, 1910.

Helm, R., ed. *Eusebius Werke. Siebenter Band. Die Chronik des Hieronymus. Hieronymi Chronicon.* GCS 47. Berlin: Akademie, 1956.

Jacoby, F. *Die Fragmente der Griechischen Historiker.* Leiden: Brill, 1957.

Karst, J., ed. and trans. *Eusebius Werke. Fünfter Band. Die Chronik aus dem Armenischen übersetzt mit textkritischen Commentar.* GCS 20. Leipzig: J. C. Hinrichs, 1911.

Klostermann, E., ed. *Eusebius Werke. III. Band 1. Hälfte. Das Onomastikon der Biblischen Ortsnamen.* GCS 11.1. Leipzig: J. C. Hinrichs, 1904.

_____, ed. *Origenes Werke. Dritter Band. Jeremiahomolien, Klageliederkommentar. Erklärung der Samuel und Königsbücher.* GCS 6. Leipzig: J. C. Hinrichs, 1901.

_____, ed. *Origenes Matthäuserklärung. II. Die lateinischen Übersetzung des commentariorum series.* GCS 38. Leipzig: J. C. Hinrichs, 1933.

_____, ed. *Origenes Werke. Zehnter Band. Origenes Matthäuserklärung.* GCS 40. Leipzig: J. C. Hinrichs, 1935.

Klostermann, E. W., ed. *Origenes Werke. Zwölfter Band. Origenes Matthäuserklärung. III. Fragmente und Indices. 1. Hälfte.* GCS 41.1. Leipzig: J. C. Hinrichs, 1941.

Koetschau, P., ed. *Origenes Werke. Erster Band. Die Schrift vom Martyrium. Buch I-IV gegen Celsus.* GCS 2. Leipzig: J. C. Hinrichs, 1899.

Krenkel, M. *Josephus und Lukas.* Leipzig, 1894.

Lange, N. R. M. de. "Jewish Influence on Origen." In *Origenia:na premier colloque international des etudes origeniennes Monserrat 18-21 Septembre 1971,* H. Crouzel, G. Lomiento and J. Rivs-Camps, 225-256, eds. Bari: University Press, 1975.

_____. *Origen and the Jews: Studies in Jewish Christian Relations in Third-Century Palestine.* Cambridge University Press, 1976.

Lightfoot, J. B. "Eusebius of Caesaria." In the *Dictionary of Christian Biography, Literature, Sects and Doctrines Being a Continuation of "The Dictionary of the Bible,"* W. Smith and H. Wace, eds. 2:308-348. London: Murray, 1880.

Maran, D. P. "Cohortatio ad Graecos." In *S. P. N. Justini* . . . PG 6:239-213. Paris, 1884.

Massebieau, L. "L'Apologetique de Tertullien et L'Octavius de Minucius Felix." *RHR15* (1887): 316-346.

Massuet, R. *S. Irenaei* . . . PG 7. Paris, 1882.

Migne, J.-P., ed. "Apologeticus Adversus Gentes Pro Christianis." In *Quinti Septimii Florentis Tertulliani* . . . PL 1:305-604. Paris, 1879.

Miller, E. *Originis Philosophoumena.* Oxford, 1851.

Monceaux, P. *Histoire litteraire de l'Afrique chretienne depuis les origines jusqu'à l'invasion arabe.* Paris: E. Leroux, 1901.

Mras, K., ed. *Eusebius Werke. Achter Band. Die Praeparatio Evangelica.* GCS 8.1-8.2. Berlin: Akademie, 1954-56.

Nautin, P. *Hippolyte et Josipe. Contribution a l'histoire de la littérature chrétienne du troisième siècle.* Paris: Les Éditions du Cerf, 1947).

_____. "La controverse sur l'auteur de l'Elenchos." *RHE* 47 (1952): 5-42.

_____. "L'Auteur du Compret Pascal de 222 et de la Chronique Anonyme de 235." *RSR* 42 (1954): 226-257.

_____. "L'homélie de 'Méliton' sur la passion." *RHE* 44 (1949): 429-438.

_____. *Le Dossier d'Hippolyte et de Méliton.* Patristica I. Paris, 1953.

Nickelsburg, G. W. E. *Resurrection, Immortality, and Eternal Life in Intertestamental Judaism.* Dissertation, Harvard University Divinity School, 1967. Pub. Cambridge, Mass.: Harvard University Press, 1972.

Niese, B., ed. *Flavii Iosephi Opera. Edidit et apparatu critico instruxit.* 6 Vols. Berlin, 1887-1895.

Otto, J. C. T., ed. *Theophili Episcopi Antiocheni. Ad Autolycum. Libri Tres.* Corpus Apologetarum Christianorum 8. Jena, 1861.

_____., ed. *Hermiae Philosphi Irrisio Gentilium Philosophorum. Apologetarum Quadrati, Aristides, Aristonis, Miltiadis, Melitonis, Apollinaris Reliquiae.* Corpus Apologetarum Christianorum 9. Jena, 1872.

Perler, O. *Ein Hymnus zur Ostervigil von Meliton? Papyrus Bodmer XII.* Paradosis 15. Freiburg: Herder, 1960.

_____. *Méliton de Sardes. Sur la Pâque et Fragments.* Sources Chrétiennes. Paris: Éditions de Cerf, 1966.

Preuschen, E., ed. *Origenes Werke. Vierter Band. Der Johanneskommentar.* GCS 10. Leipzig: J. C. Hinrichs, 1903.

Richard, M. "Comput et chronographie chez S. Hippolyte." *MScR* 7 (1950): 237-268.

_____. "Comput et chronographie chez S. Hippolyte." *MScR* 8 (1951): 19-50.

_____. "Encore la Problème D'Hippolyte." *MScR* 10 (1953): 13-52 and 145-180.

Schoedel, W. R. "Philosophy and Rhetoric in the *Adversus Haereses* of Irenaeus." *VC* 13 (1959): 27-31.

Schreckenberg, H. *Die Flavius-Josephus-Tradition in Antike und Mittelalter.* Leiden: Brill, 1972.

_____. *Rezeptionsgeschichte und textkritische Untersuchungen zu Flavius Josephus.* Leiden: Brill, 1977.

Schwartz, E., ed. *Eusebius Werke. Zweiter Band. Die Kirchengeschichte.* GCS 9.3. Leipzig: J. C. Hinrichs, 1909.

_____ and T. Mommsen, eds. *Eusebius Werke. Zweiter Band. Die Kirchengeschichte. Die Lateinische Übersetzung des Rufinus.* GCS 9.1-9.3. Leipzig: J. C. Hinrichs, 1903-1909.

Schürer, E. "Julius Africanus als Quelle der Pseudo-Justin'schen Cohortatio ad Graecos." *ZKG* 2 (1877-78): 319-331.

Smith, M. "The Description of the Essenes in Josephus and the Philosophoumena." *HUCA* 29 (1958): 273-313.

Stählin, O., ed. *Clemens Alexandrinus. Zweiter Band. Stromata Buch I-VI.* GCS 15. Leipzig: J. C. Hinrichs, 1906.

_____, ed. *Clemens Alexandrinus. Dritter Band. Stromata Buch VII und VIII. Excerpta ex Theodoto–Eclogai Propheticae Quis Dives Salvetur–Fragmente.* GCS 17. Leipzig: J. C. Hinrichs, 1909.

_____ and L. Früchtel, eds. *Clemens Alexandrinus. Zweiter Band. Stromata Buch I-VI.* 3rd ed. GCS 52. Berlin: Akademie, 1960.

Testuz, M., ed. *Papyrus Bodmer XIII, Méliton de Sardes Homélie sur la Pâque.* Bibliotheca Bodmeriana. Geneva, 1960.

Thackeray, H. St. J., ed. and trans. *Josephus. The Life. Against Apion.* LCL. London: Heinemann and Cambridge, Mass.: Harvard University Press, 1926.

_____, trans. *Selections from Josephus.* London: S.P.C.K., 1919.

Timothy, H. B. *The Early Christian Apologists and Greek Philosophy Exemplified by Irenaeus, Tertullian and Clement of Alexandria.* Assen: Van Gorcum, 1973.

Torrey, C. C. *The Composition and Date of Acts.* Cambridge, Mass.: Harvard University Press, 1916.

Völter, D. "Über Zeit und Verfasser des pseudo-justinischen Cohortatio ad Graecos." *ZWT* 26 (1883): 180-215.

Wacholder, B. Z. *Eupolemos. A Study of Judeo-Greek Literature.* Cincinnati: Hebrew Union College Press, 1974.

Weber, Karl-Otto. *Origenes der Neuplatoniker: Versuch einer Interpretation.* München: C. H. Beck, 1962.

Wendland, Paul, ed. *Hippolytus Werke. Dritter Band. Refutatio omnium haeresium.* GCS 26. Leipzig: J. C. Hinrichs, 1916.

Wilhelm, F. "De Min. Fel. Oct. et Tert. Apol." *Breslauer philol. Abhandl.* 2.1. Breslau, 1887.

Winter, Paul. "Excursus II–Josephus on Jesus and James *Ant.* xviii, 3, 3 (63-4) and xx 9, 1 (200-3)." In E. Schürer's *The History of the Jewish People in the Age of Jesus Christ,* G. Vermes, F. Millar and M. Black, eds. 1:428-441. Edinburgh: T. & T. Clark, 1973.

Zeitlin, S. "The Account of the Essenes in Josephus and the Philosophoumenu." *JQR* 59 (1958-59): 292-299.

Zoepfl, F. *Der Kommentar des Pseudo-Eustathios zum Hexaëmeron.* Münster i.W., 1927.

Index

Josephan Citations

18.237 80

18.252 80

18.255 80

18.257-260 80

19.343-351 122

19.346 82

20.97-98 83, 121, 122

20.97-102 61, 107

20.101 83

20.169 86

20.180-181 86, 123

20.197 83

20.199-203 83

20.200 60

20.238 75

20.257 86

20.267 75

20.268 75

B.J.

1.3 74

1.123 76

1.181 76

1.664 77

1.656-660 76

1.668-669 77

2.93-94 77

2.115 50, 112

2.118 77

2.119 54

2.119-166 53

2.148 55

2.150 80

2.162 54

2.169 61

2.204 82

2.211 77

2.156-170 122

2.169 108, 116

2.169-170 81

2.175-177 81

2.227 86

2.247-248 86

2.254-256 123

2.261-263 86, 123

2.284 123

2.306-308 123

2.461 86

2.461-465 123

2.465 87

3.399 87

4.335-344 61, 108, 116

4.491 87

4.658 87

5.424-438 88

5.442-445 88

5.446 116

5.512-519 88

5.566 88

6.193-213 17, 88

6.199 208 88

6.201-213 116

6.288-304 90

6.299 62, 64, 116

6.312-313 90, 124

6.417 89

6.418 89

6.420 89

6.426 88

6.435 31, 66

6.435-437 65, 108, 117

C.A.

1.6-14 94
1.14 50, 112
1.15-16 94
1.19-21 94
1.22 95
1.23-26 95
1.38-42 94
1.73-75 100
1.73-105 100
1.82-90 100
1.93-102 11, 106
1.94-103 13
1.103-105 100
1.103-126 106
1.106-127 100
1.104 11, 49
1.108 100
1.111 49,
1.117-126 13
1.126 100
1.127 11, 12, 107
1.128-134 99
1.128-154 11, 107
1.134-141 12
1.136-137 99

1.146-153 99
1.155-160 100
1.172-174 99
1.176-179 99
1.197-204 98
2.1 49
2.8-144 49
2.19 32
2.163-167 91
2.168-171 91
2.171-178 91
2.179-189 92
2.183 120
2.193-198 92
2.195 49
2.199-203 92
2.204 92
2.205 93
2.206-208 93
2.209-214 93
2.215-217 93
2.217-219 93
2.220-228 94

V.

361 75

Brown Judaic Studies

Brown Studies on Jews and Their Societies

Brown Studies in Religion